EXTRAORDINARY LIFE PLANNER

SIX COMMITMENTS TO LIVE YOUR DREAMS & CHANGE YOUR WORLD

YOUR EXTRAORDINARY LIFE PLAN
LIVE YOUR DREAMS & CHANGE YOUR WORLD

Merriam Webster's Dictionary defines "extraordinary" as going beyond what is usual, regular or customary. Exceptional to a very marked extent.

This guide has been designed to walk you through the step-by-step strategies to design and live your very own extraordinary life. If you invest the time to complete it and put it into action your results will be staggering! Many others have used this process to live successful, fulfilled and extraordinary lives so let's get into action and increase your clarity, motivation and focus on exactly what you need to do to create a breakthrough in your life!

By embracing The Six Extraordinary Commitments included in this guide you will realize your dreams and change your world faster than you ever thought possible!

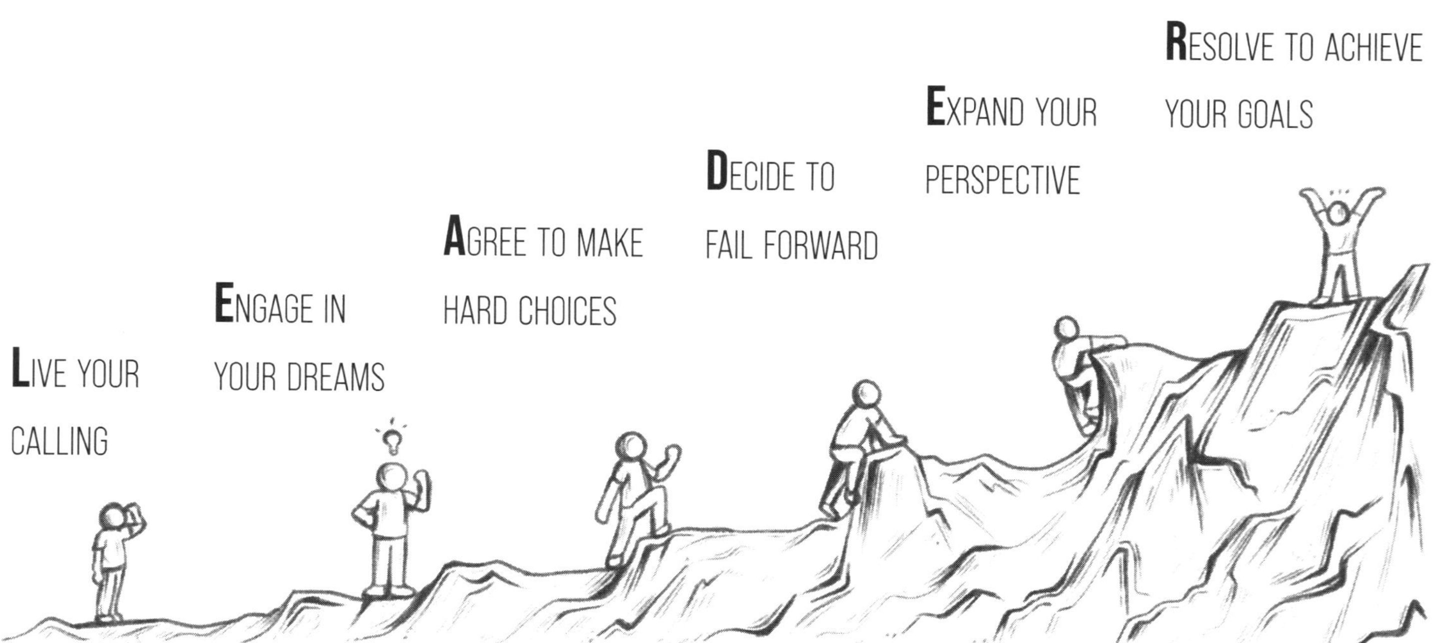

EXTRAORDINARY LIFE ASSESSMENT

WHERE TO START?
COMPLETE THE EXTRAORDINARY LIFE ASSESSMENT

Complete the assessment by assigning a value 1 to 10 (10 being the best you could possibly do) in each of the following areas:

PHYSICAL WELL-BEING

Healthy weight	1
Nutrition Habits (eating a balanced nutrition plan with healthy foods)	____
Hydration Habits (Drinking 80 oz. of water daily)	____
Energy Management (Sleeping well, energized and rested)	7
Fitness Habits (exercising regularly, staying active 30 minutes or more daily)	5
No medications (for lifestyle-related diseases)	8
Physical Well-Being Score: (add all the above scores here)	____

MENTAL WELL-BEING

Handle stress well	____
Time for family and friends	____
Happy and fulfilled	____
Enjoying career (or retirement)	____
Spiritually healthy	____
Pursuing hobbies and other interests	____
Mental Well-Being Score: (add all the above scores here)	____

FINANCIAL/VOCATION WELL-BEING

Enjoying Career/Business and work environment	____
Debt free	____
Savings for emergencies	____
Retirement fund	____
Abundance of time and money to contribute to worthy causes	____
Fun cash for vacations, hobbies, entertainment	____
Financial Well-Being Total Score: (add all the above scores here)	____

COMBINED TOTAL SCORE FROM ALL THREE CATEGORIES: ____

(physical/mental/financial)

EXTRAORDINARY LIFE ASSESSMENT

ORDINARY LIFE RIVER RAFTERS

This group is filled with multitudes of people just going with the flow, floating through life, enjoying immediate gratification, pursuing the path of least resistance. They choose not to do anything extraordinary because they either lack knowledge about what's possible or allow fear, doubt, and limiting beliefs to squash faith in their ability to rise above their circumstances and achieve something extraordinary.

Their focus on the here and now keeps them from seeing the benefits of pursuing the extraordinary. Not only that, but the longer they stay in the river, the greater the chance these ***River Rafters*** will go over the ***Waterfall of Life***, a perilous cascade that includes significant failures, regrets, lifestyle-related diseases, relationship issues, and even premature death.

Unfortunately, this group constitutes most of the world's population. Their health, financial statement, education, and life are dictated by their lack of a dream, lack of skills, unhealthy habits, and poor decision-making.

VALLEY DWELLERS

This group is filled with complacent people who do not consciously choose either failure or success. They are indecisive and fearful of the consequences of change. They live what they may call the "good life" but often complain about their circumstances. They blame their hardships on others and feel victimized by someone else's choices. They may have a "good" job and average relationships with family and friends. They're not sick but also not healthy. They may have a retirement account, but not one that allows them to live the life they've dreamt about.

Valley Dwellers take short vacations, focus on the cost of everything, and dread going back to work on Mondays after a short weekend of relaxation. They don't love what they do and rarely, if ever, experience the excitement of achieving something truly extraordinary, daring, challenging, or exciting.

These ***Valley Dwellers*** often lack the thrill of striving for big dreams and something truly EXTRAordinary. They occasionally raft ***Ordinary Life River*** to bring some immediate gratification and make risky choices, but they descend back into the valley when they begin to experience the pains and consequences associated with their choices just before they go over the ***Waterfall of Life***.

Valley Dwellers often stay away from climbing ***Extraordinary Life Mountain*** because of what their family and friends may think if they choose to strive for something extraordinary. Or, they refrain from doing something extraordinary due to a lack of belief in themselves or lack of a dream, mission, or calling. In doing so, they remain trapped between a failing and ***Extraordinary Life***.

COMFORT CAVE CAMPERS

People in this group have experienced some level of extraordinary results and success in life but have become comfortable with their achievements. They stopped pursuing the extraordinary and they are living their life focused on past achievements versus challenging themselves to learn more, become more, and achieve more. ***Comfort Cave Campers*** are filled with talents, gifts, strengths, good health, and the capacity to do so much more to make a huge impact in the world but opt for comfort over significance.

Cave Campers often feel motivated and called to take risks, embrace new challenges, or dream bigger but don't because of the effort, sacrifice, and investment of time and energy required. Or, they fear failure and a potential hit to their ego. When they think about chasing a new dream and climbing a new peak, the motivation passes and remaining comfortable takes priority. This group has the greatest of untapped potential.

EXTRAORDINARY LIFE CLIFF CLIMBERS

These are the people who live the most extraordinary lives. They constantly strive to reach new peaks of success and significance. They discover and live their calling, realize their dreams, achieve their goals, pioneer new ideas, and create products, experiences, solutions, and businesses to better the lives of others. The world watches this group of leaders live a life filled with adventure, mystery, purpose, and excitement. They turn the impossible into the possible. They show up when others don't. They are often labeled by others as foolish, dreamers, daredevils, or the crazy ones. They are often ridiculed, laughed at, and mocked by the ***River***

Rafters and *Valley Dwellers* because they don't know what they don't know until they see what they never saw. *Extraordinary Life Cliff Climbers* are remembered long after they die thanks to their heroic efforts, inventions, leadership, and accomplishments.

Being an *Extraordinary Life Cliff Climber* is not for everyone. It is reserved for those who do not accept the status quo and are willing to put in the EXTRA effort, time, sacrifice, and resources to achieve extraordinary results, success, and significance in whatever they feel called to be, do, or have. Becoming an *Extraordinary Life Cliff Climber* is for those who consciously choose to take risks, make sacrifices, and leave lasting legacies for future generations to follow.

"PEOPLE DO NOT DECIDE TO BECOME EXTRAORDINARY. THEY DECIDE TO ACCOMPLISH EXTRAORDINARY THINGS."

- SIR EDMUND HILLARY, THE FIRST PERSON TO SUMMIT MOUNT EVEREST

Sir Edmund Percival Hillary, a New Zealand mountaineer, explorer, and philanthropist, reached the top of Mount Everest, the highest mountain in the world, standing at 29,029 feet, on May 29, 1953. Hillary, who was thirty-three at the time, was accompanied by Nepalese Sherpa mountaineer Tenzing Norgay. The two became the first climbers known to summit Mount Everest and were regarded as the world's preeminent mountaineers.

In an interview following their ascent, Hillary was asked why he decided to climb the mountain. He responded, "I didn't climb the mountain to conquer the mountain. I did it to conquer myself."

Since Hillary and Norgay's ascent, there have been over five thousand successful summit attempts of Everest by climbers worldwide. That means more than five thousand people have conquered themselves because two men decided to do something extraordinary and be the first to reach Mount Everest's peak. This list includes Erik Weihenmayer in 2001 (who is blind), Mark Inglis in 2006 (a double amputee), and Jordan Romero in 2010 (who was only thirteen years old at the time).

When we identify something extraordinary, it becomes the mountain peak we are destined and determined to conquer. Imagine for just a moment how exciting and meaningful your life would be if you chose to pursue an extraordinary calling, mission, dream, or goal that was significant to you, and you conquered it.

Whether you are a ***River Rafter, Valley Dweller, Comfort Cave Camper,*** or ***Cliff Climber*** right now does not define your ability to change your life, nor does it define you as a person. What matters most is, do you want to live ***an Extraordinary Life,*** and are you willing to commit to making it happen? We need more leaders who will no longer accept the ordinary as our everyday reality. We need to grow ourselves into leaders who will live extraordinary lives and deliver extraordinary results.

The opportunity is here for a new American Revolution—a revolution against complacency and the ordinary life. You can choose to answer the call and live an ***Extraordinary Life*** or ignore it altogether. I believe we all have the power to change the course of events. When enough of us have the same belief, our country (and our lives) will change for the better.

This book reveals the step-by-step strategies and ***Six Extraordinary Commitments*** that many ordinary people have used to become ***Extraordinary Life Cliff Climbers*** and live successful, fulfilled, extraordinary lives.

HOW DID YOU SCORE?

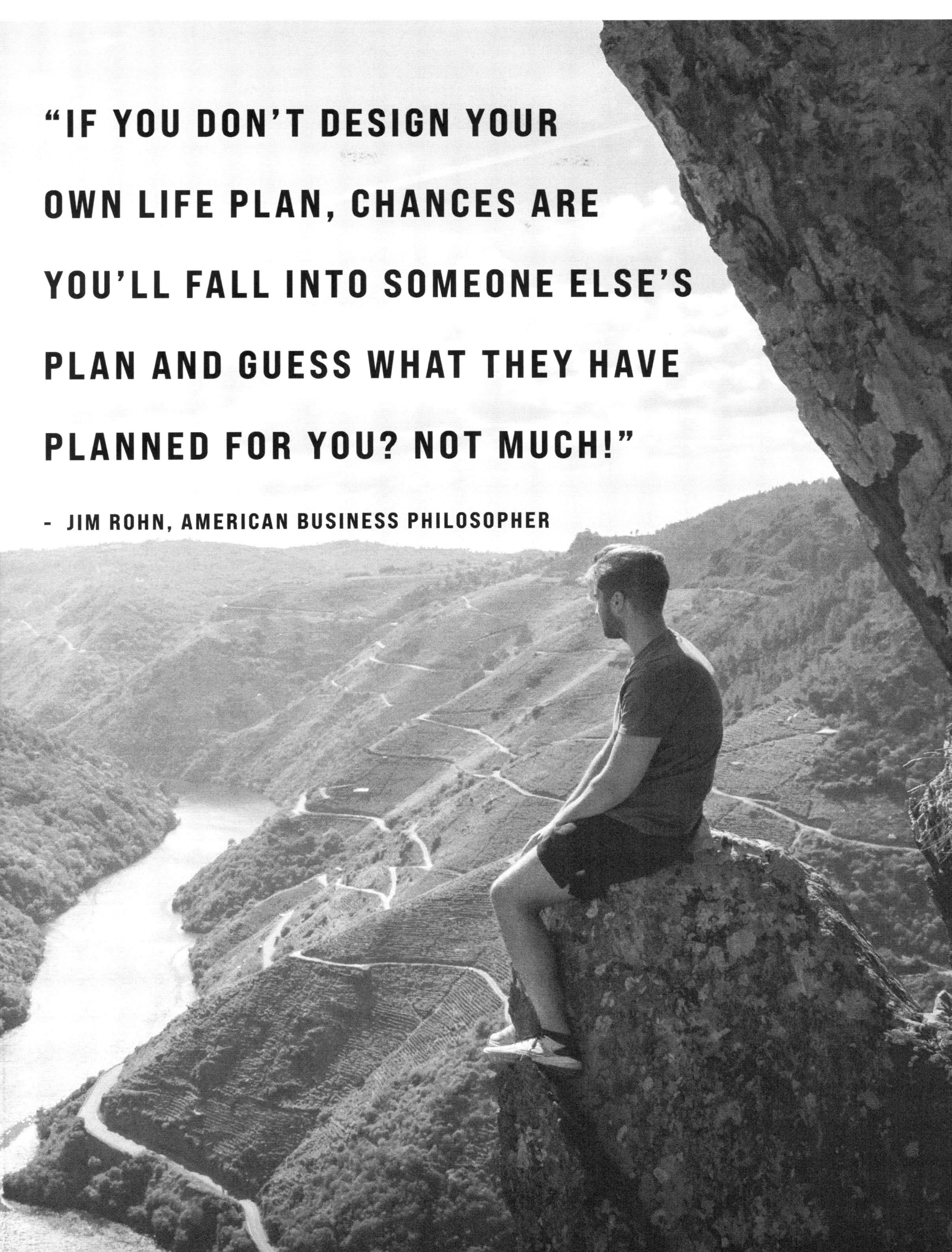
"IF YOU DON'T DESIGN YOUR OWN LIFE PLAN, CHANCES ARE YOU'LL FALL INTO SOMEONE ELSE'S PLAN AND GUESS WHAT THEY HAVE PLANNED FOR YOU? NOT MUCH!"
- JIM ROHN, AMERICAN BUSINESS PHILOSOPHER

COMMITMENT # 1: LIVE YOUR CALLING

History has proven those who live an extraordinary life come in all colors, shapes, and sizes, yet they share common commitments, the first of which is to LIVE YOUR CALLING.

Every great leader answers a call. Some responded to a call from another leader in their life; others responded to an inner calling that challenged them to go beyond the status quo.

These leaders chose to live out their calling and/or answer the call to live an extraordinary life day after day, week after week, month after month, year after year. That is how an extraordinary life is lived and a remarkable legacy is achieved.

Unfortunately, many people want to live The Extraordinary Life but have a list of reasons as to why they can't answer the call, such as fear, doubt, uncertainty, busyness, insufficient finances, lack of support or time, as to why they can't answer the call. They decide not to take the time to identify their true calling in life and become comfortable with their ordinary lives. These people often suffer regrets, depression and boredom in life because they don't have anything calling them to get uncomfortable.

Let's start the Extraordinary Life Planning process by answering some thought provoking questions that will help you clarify your calling.

What do you (or your family and friends) believe are your three greatest strengths, talents, gifts or qualities? Vocational, Hobby, Interests

What specific activities bring you the most joy and fulfillment?

Teaching, reading, writing, speaking

If time and money weren't an issue and you could do anything you wanted, what would you do with your time?

COMMITMENT # 1: LIVE YOUR CALLING

What breaks your heart? Who do you want to help? Do you have a group of individuals you are naturally most concerned about (i.e. orphans, single moms, those who are unhealthy, the poor, addicted, hungry, abused, those who lack purpose, etc.)?

What would you like your gravestone to read?

What type of legacy would you like to leave after you die?
What do you want to be remembered for?

What are your answers to these questions showing you?

Where do you see a calling in your life?

Why do you think you exist here on earth? What do you sense you're "called" to do or be?

"HAVE YOU BUILT YOUR CASTLES IN THE SKY? GOOD, THAT IS WHERE THEY SHOULD BE. NOW BUILD THE FOUNDATIONS UNDERNEATH THEM."

- HENRY DAVID THOREAU

COMMITMENT # 2: ENGAGE IN YOUR DREAMS

Clarifying your dreams and defining what you want to be, do and have can be a challenging exercise for some. Webster's Dictionary defines the word focus as "the center of activity, attraction or attention. A point of concentration."

Are you focused on a point of concentration in your life? Until we can become intentional about achieving this type of clarity, we will feel like we're lost; and we won't yet have a clear understanding of where we are going.

When we were children, focusing on our dreams may have been much easier. We could dream about our future without the fear, doubt and negative influences we may have now or the pain of past failures that often keep us from trying something again or something new. However, with just a little practice and a growth mindset, we can reclaim that childlike focus and curiosity whenever we choose!

For the next few minutes, I want you to think about getting into a helicopter to take an aerial view of your entire life. What is it that you see as you look down on your career, relationships, finances and health? What is happening as you look at your life from 5,000 feet?

BEGIN DREAMING ABOUT YOUR EXTRAORDINARY LIFE!

What would you like to see happen during your lifetime? What do you see yourself achieving? What do you intend to do "in your life" and "with your life"? What kind of impact would you like to make because of your life? Dream about the possibilities and don't worry if it sounds impossible based on your current circumstances.

COMMITMENT # 2: ENGAGE IN YOUR DREAMS

PHYSICAL WELL-BEING

How would you describe your current physical health?

Describe how you would define extraordinary health and what it would look like in your life?

What would you like to lose, gain, quit or start doing consistently regarding your physical health?

I will Weigh ________lbs Get to________ % body fat Wear a size ________

Other Physical Dreams:

- [ ] Run or walk a 5k or 10k race
- [ ] Run a half marathon, marathon or triathlon
- [ ] ______________________________
- [ ] ______________________________

COMMITMENT # 2: ENGAGE IN YOUR DREAMS

CAREER/BUSINESS/FINANCIAL WELL-BEING

What would your ideal business/career look like if you could do anything? What would you like to be (business owner, position or title), do (responsibilities) and have (specifically)?

What are your financial dreams?

What amount of income would make you smile?

If money wasn't an issue, what would you splurge on?

Do you want to retire from working altogether? If so, when? ____________________

COMMITMENT # 2: ENGAGE IN YOUR DREAMS

MENTAL WELL-BEING

What relationships would you like to start, improve or eliminate? And why?

Who do you want to spend more time with? And why?

What would bring you more peace of mind, purpose and fulfillment? And why?

What do you want to learn, become and understand more?

COMMITMENT # 2: ENGAGE IN YOUR DREAMS

Do You Want to Add Any of These Adventures to Your Life?
(Check the box of each activity you'd like to experience)

- [ ] Learn a new language
- [ ] Learn to play an instrument
- [ ] See a Broadway Play
- [ ] Go zip lining
- [ ] Learn to dance
- [ ] Go backpacking
- [ ] Start your own business
- [ ] Write a book
- [x] Ride a motorcycle (cross-country)
- [ ] Go snowmobiling
- [ ] Play paintball
- [ ] Go hang gliding
- [ ] Ride in a helicopter
- [ ] Go white water river rafting
- [ ] Fly first class
- [ ] Ride in a hot air balloon
- [ ] Play in a waterfall
- [ ] Be part of a flash mob
- [x] Drive Route 66 (on a Touring Motorbike)
- [ ] Go cliff jumping
- [ ] Go ice skating
- [ ] Go indoor skydiving
- [ ] Go Jet Skiing
- [ ] Go kitesurfing or kiteboarding
- [x] Go on a road trip with a friend
- [ ] Go camping
- [ ] Go mountain biking
- [x] Go paragliding
- [ ] Go sand surfing
- [x] Go water skiing
- [x] Go windsurfing
- [ ] Plant a tree
- [ ] Sleep underneath the stars
- [ ] Solve a Rubik's Cube
- [ ] Watch a meteor shower
- [ ] Climb a rock wall
- [ ] Drive a dune buggy
- [x] Go Sky diving
- [ ] Go SCUBA diving
- [x] Go bungee jumping
- [ ] Ride a Segway, horse, camel, elephant
- [ ] Swim with dolphins/whales/sharks
- [x] Race cars on a track
- [ ] Go to a rodeo
- [x] Watch a TV show live (Price Is Right)
- [ ] Climb a mountain
- [ ] Go to a TED conference
- [ ] Go on a major cruise
- [ ] Go racing at Talladega
- [ ] Go to the World Series
- [x] Go to the Super Bowl
- [x] Go to Olympics Opening Ceremonies
- [ ] Go to Olympics events live
- [ ] Go to a PGA Tour event
- [x] Attend a Kentucky Derby
- [ ] Get autograph and picture with (name of celebrity or athlete) ______________________
- [ ] See a Vegas show
- [ ] Watch a [artist or band name] concert live
- [ ] See one game at every baseball stadium
- [x] See one game at every football stadium

COMMITMENT # 2: ENGAGE IN YOUR DREAMS

- [ ] See one game at every [sport] stadium ______________________
- [ ] Watch a Wimbledon championship match
- [ ] Watch a WWE match live
- [ ] Watch an NBA All-Star Weekend live
- [ ] Watch the world's best fireworks displays
- [ ] Watch an exhibition by the US Air Force Thunderbirds
- [ ] Watch an opera
- [ ] Watch world-class symphony orchestra perform
- [ ] Watch a live ballet performance of the Swan Lake
- [ ] Watch all [film director's name] films ______________________
- [ ] Learn how to play [name of sports] ______________________
- [ ] Learn archery
- [ ] Learn how to play chess
- [ ] Learn how to snowboard
- [ ] Learn how to ice-skate
- [ ] Learn to ski
- [ ] Learn to surf
- [ ] Learn Taekwondo/Aikido/Jujitsu/Karate
- [ ] Learn how to cook [name of dish] ______________________
- [ ] Learn how to bake [name of cake or pastry] ______________________
- [ ] Learn how to speak [name of languages] ______________________
- [ ] Learn how to play [name of games] ______________________
- [ ] Learn how to play poker
- [x] Learn to fly
- [ ] Learn how to ride a horse
- [x] Learn how to ride a motorcycle
- [ ] Learn how to shoot a gun
- [x] Increase your photography skills
- [ ] Learn sign language
- [ ] Learn to juggle
- [ ] Learn to knit or sew
- [ ] Learn to speed read
- [ ] Learn how to cross-stitch
- [ ] Learn how to play the guitar
- [ ] Learn public speaking
- [ ] Learn how to meditate
- [ ] Learn self-defense
- [ ] Learn how to budget
- [ ] Become an expert in [name of field or industry] ______________________
- [ ] Learn at least _____ magic tricks
- [ ] Learn how to blow glass
- [ ] Learn how to practice mindfulness
- [ ] Learn how to make a sculpture
- [ ] Get married
- [ ] Become a parent
- [ ] Adopt and raise a child
- [ ] Be a bridesmaid/groomsman
- [x] Get a bachelor's or master's degree or PhD
- [x] Become debt-free
- [ ] Buy an investment property
- [ ] Buy a brand-new car
- [ ] Become a millionaire by [age] ________
- [ ] Live and/or study abroad for [time period] ______________________
- [ ] Join a specific ministry in church

COMMITMENT # 2: ENGAGE IN YOUR DREAMS

Places to visit: (List the countries and check the states you'd like to visit or experience)

- [ ] Alabama
- [ ] Alaska
- [ ] Arizona
- [ ] Arkansas
- [ ] California
- [ ] Colorado
- [ ] Connecticut
- [ ] Delaware
- [ ] Florida
- [ ] Georgia
- [ ] Hawaii
- [ ] Idaho
- [ ] Illinois
- [ ] Indiana
- [ ] Iowa
- [ ] Kansas
- [ ] Kentucky
- [ ] Louisiana
- [ ] Maine
- [ ] Maryland
- [ ] Massachusetts
- [ ] Michigan
- [ ] Minnesota
- [ ] Mississippi
- [ ] Missouri
- [ ] Montana
- [ ] Nebraska
- [ ] Nevada
- [ ] New Hampshire
- [ ] New Jersey
- [ ] New Mexico
- [ ] New York
- [ ] North Carolina
- [ ] North Dakota
- [ ] Ohio
- [ ] Oklahoma
- [ ] Oregon
- [ ] Pennsylvania
- [ ] Rhode Island
- [ ] South Carolina
- [ ] South Dakota
- [ ] Tennessee
- [ ] Texas
- [ ] Utah
- [ ] Vermont
- [ ] Virginia
- [ ] Washington
- [ ] West Virginia
- [ ] Wisconsin
- [ ] Wyoming

Countries I'd want to visit:

______________________ ______________________ ______________________

______________________ ______________________ ______________________

______________________ ______________________ ______________________

______________________ ______________________ ______________________

"YOU'LL ACCOMPLISH YOUR DREAMS ONLY WHEN YOU HAVE ENOUGH REASONS TO ACCOMPLISH THEM BECAUSE WHEN THE WHY GETS STRONGER, THE HOW GETS EASIER."

– JIM ROHN

COMMITMENT # 3: AGREE TO MAKE HARD CHOICES

It is good to have big dreams prioritized into a timeline, but that isn't all you need to make those dreams come true.

You need to be willing to agree to make hard choices. You need to say no to some activities and yes to other activities that stretch you. These activities are often the ones we don't necessarily want to do but they are required to making our dreams come true.

Just as we need architectural drawings when constructing a building or a road map when traveling to an unknown destination, we need sound action plans if we hope to live our biggest dreams.

Our dreams require action plans to help us break them down into smaller (and more achievable) goals and action steps, so we don't get overwhelmed with the magnitude of the dream.

Without a solid action plan, we may never achieve anything we really want in life; we may end up wandering aimlessly, like countless dreamers who have lost their way. Some people prefer to wander without a plan because they think developing one is tedious. Actually, wandering aimlessly as a way of life often leads to a life filled with regrets!

If we lack an action plan, we may easily get lost, led astray or become discouraged. A good action plan will alleviate all this uncertainty and give us a clear sense of direction each and every day.

Just like a road map or GPS navigation system gives us a clear sense of direction when driving toward a desired destination, an action plan can do the same for our big dream(s).

WHAT'S INSIDE AN ACTION PLAN?

A SOLID ACTION PLAN CONSISTS OF THREE ITEMS:

- A Purpose Statement
- S.M.A.R.T. Goals
- Action Steps

The Purpose Statement is the reason(s) you want to realize your dream. What would realizing the dream do for you? Upon successfully achieving the dream, what benefits would you experience? By writing these REASONS down, you'll be reminded of them each time you review your action plan.

COMMITMENT # 3: AGREE TO MAKE HARD CHOICES

S. M. A. R. T. goals break your dream down into specific, measurable, achievable, realistic, and time-sensitive targets. Action steps are the specific activities you will undertake to support those S. M. A. R. T. goals—activities you'll want to review and refine regularly. Just thinking about your goals is not enough. You must act!

With all three elements in place, you'll be able to chart your course and measure your performance in accomplishing the big dream. You will also have something concrete and achievable each day to focus your energy on. There's an old phrase: "How do you eat an elephant? One bite at a time." If you follow this philosophy, you will be on the right path.

"ONE HOUR OF PLANNING IS EQUAL TO EIGHT HOURS OF HARD LABOR."

– BENJAMIN FRANKLIN

You have a choice: Plan now and work less or plan later (or maybe not at all) and work more. Remember, the shortest distance between you and your dream is a straight line. The more complete your plan, the straighter the line. Once you create your plan, proceed to the next section to learn how to strengthen your commitment to carry it out and realize your dreams!

IMPORTANT QUESTIONS TO CONSIDER FOR YOUR PLAN

What goal would get me closer to this dream?

What do I need to do today or this week to better realize this dream?

What action will I take today?

"HE WHO EVERY MORNING PLANS THE TRANSACTION OF THE DAY AND FOLLOWS OUT THAT PLAN, CARRIES A THREAD THAT WILL GUIDE HIM THROUGH THE MAZE OF THE MOST BUSY LIFE. BUT WHERE NO PLAN IS LAID, WHERE THE DISPOSAL OF TIME IS SURRENDERED MERELY TO THE CHANCE OF INCIDENCE, CHAOS WILL SOON REIGN."

- VICTOR HUGO, FRENCH POET, PLAYWRIGHT, AND HUMAN RIGHTS ACTIVIST

MY EXTRAORDINARY PHYSICAL WELLNESS PLAN

What is your specific desired outcome? Clarify your dream(s).

When would you like to achieve it? (Due date) ______________________________

Why would you like to achieve it? (Motivational reasons, benefits of achievement)

How will you achieve it?

Goal: ____ Due Date: __________

Action Step: ____ Due Date: __________

Goal: ____ Due Date: __________

Action Step: ____ Due Date: __________

Goal: ____ Due Date: __________

Action Step: ____ Due Date: __________

Who will help you achieve it? __________________________ __________________________

__________________________ __________________________

Where are you now? (Be specific about the details, the pain/problems, etc.)

MY EXTRAORDINARY MENTAL WELLNESS PLAN

What is your specific desired outcome? Clarify your dream(s).

When would you like to achieve it? (Due date) ______________________________

Why would you like to achieve it? (Motivational reasons, benefits of achievement)

How will you achieve it?

Goal: ______________________________ Due Date: __________

Action Step: ______________________________ Due Date: __________

Goal: ______________________________ Due Date: __________

Action Step: ______________________________ Due Date: __________

Goal: ______________________________ Due Date: __________

Action Step: ______________________________ Due Date: __________

Who will help achieve it? ____________________ ____________________

____________________ ____________________

Where are you now? (Be specific about the details, the pain/problems, etc.)

MY EXTRAORDINARY FINANCIAL WELLNESS PLAN

What is your specific desired outcome? Clarify your dream(s).

When would you like to achieve it? (Due date) ______________________________

Why would you like to achieve it? (Motivational reasons, benefits of achievement)

How will you achieve it?

Goal: ____ Due Date: __________

Action Step: ____ Due Date: __________

Goal: ____ Due Date: __________

Action Step: ____ Due Date: __________

Goal: ____ Due Date: __________

Action Step: ____ Due Date: __________

Who will help achieve it? __________________________ __________________________

__________________________ __________________________

Where are you now? (Be specific about the details, the pain/problems, etc.)

"WE WOULD ACCOMPLISH MANY MORE THINGS IF WE DID NOT THINK OF THEM AS IMPOSSIBLE."

- VINCE LOMBARDI

COMMITMENT # 4: DECIDE TO FAIL FORWARD

IMPLEMENTING OUR PLANS AND ACTING ON OUR DREAMS USUALLY COMES DOWN TO THREE THINGS:

- Getting motivated and inspired enough to take the initiative;
- Maintaining that motivation and inspiration despite the failures and setbacks; and
- Deciding to fail forward.

How do you motivate yourself to tackle your biggest dreams?

Do you have a plan in place to stay motivated even when things don't go as planned? You should! The best way is to be active in accomplishing tasks that move you closer to your dream. You can also stay motivated by renewing your mind with positive, inspirational resources, such as books, podcasts, videos, Bible verses, inspirational quotes and similar materials.

There are days when staying motivated is hard for even the most extraordinary leaders. Most of us require the assistance of others. There are times when we don't feel like tackling a new dream (or staying persistent with an old one that hasn't come true yet). Motivation comes and goes. In fact, motivation comes quickly and leaves even more unexpectedly than it arrived! We hear a song that motivates us to do something special and an hour later, we forgot what it was that moved us. We attend a seminar and get energized entirely to make a change in our life and take copious notes on all changes we're going to make. The next day, we can't even find our notes!

We are so bombarded with forces competing for our attention—advertisements, phone calls, kids, work, and so on—that often, the urgent outweighs the essential and something called the Law of Declining Intent takes over.

The Law of Declining Intent says if you fail to act on an idea the moment you are motivated to do so, the odds of you ever acting begin to decline rapidly from that point forward.

HOW DO WE OVERCOME THIS?

1. Act immediately on whatever it is you feel inspired to do. Begin developing your action plan for the weight you want to lose, business you want to start or trip you want to take—and do it now! Action is an internal motivator that inspires you to take more action.

2. Invest in yourself and purchase resources you can use consistently to regain motivation whenever it lapses. These may be books, movies, audio and video programs, podcasts, blogs or music that changes your emotional state. Good books are essential!

Extraordinary leaders are extraordinary readers; they know if they grow mentally, they will grow personally and professionally.

3. Ask someone to hold you accountable for whatever you need the motivation to do. Make a promise to yourself about how you plan to take action, then share it with your spouse, significant other or trusted friend. You'll be more motivated to execute your plan!

4. Decide to Fail Forward. When something doesn't go as planned, identify what happened, what you wanted to happen, what you feel is missing and decide what your next action is to move you closer to your dreams and goals.

5. Plan your priorities. We're all given 24 precious hours per day, no more and no less. We must become crystal clear about the priorities we set for those hours. Let's act on our highest priorities first and leave all minor priorities to whatever time is leftover. Only then will our time management efforts be successful. If we approach things haphazardly or ignore high-priority items in favor of low-priority ones, we won't get much traction on our goals.

Begin managing your priorities by scheduling your highest into your daily calendar. Use the table on the following page to assist you in planning your Extraordinary Life. Use the words that start with the letter "F" to guide you to schedule appointments with yourself so you can invest the needed time for your faith, fitness, family, friendships, fun and the most important tasks in your firm or career. Be vigilant with the appointments you schedule with yourself. When you hit a bump in the road—which you will—keep your priorities in place, no matter how dire the emergency seems. Find a way to prioritize the problem... then schedule a time to act on it!

PRIORITY MANAGEMENT
(BLOCK OUT TIME FOR THE 7 F'S)

TIME	MON.	TUE.	WED.	THURS.	FRI.	SAT.	SUN.
5:00AM							
5:30AM							
6:00AM							
6:30AM							
7:00AM							
7:30AM							
8:00AM							
8:30AM							
9:00AM							
9:30AM							
10:00AM							
10:30AM							
11:00AM							
11:30AM							
12:00PM							
12:30PM							
1:00PM							
1:30PM							
2:00PM							
2:30PM							
3:00PM							
3:30PM							
4:00PM							
4:30PM							
5:00PM							
5:30PM							
6:00PM							
6:30PM							
7:00PM							
7:30PM							
8:00PM							
8:30PM							
9:00PM							
9:30PM							

FAITH FAMILY FINANCES FIRM FITNESS FRIENDS FUN

COMMITMENT # 5: EXPAND YOUR PERSPECTIVE

"ACCOUNTABILITY BREEDS RESPONSE-ABILITY."

- STEPHEN COVEY, BEST SELLING AUTHOR

Extraordinary athletes have coaches to help them get extraordinary results. Leaders who want to go beyond what is usual, regular, and customary in their lives also need coaches who can take them farther than they can take themselves.

Why is having a coach so important? A coach brings some critical pieces to the success puzzle you will not find anywhere else:

- Strategic perspective, insights, and knowledge different from your own, along with the ability to identify "blind spots" you cannot see;
- Resources, tools, and tactics to help one accomplish the mission in less time with less effort and mistakes; and
- Accountability, motivation, and encouragement to help us go beyond what is comfortable.

Once someone has reached the peak of success with the help of a coach, you will find that person rarely takes on a major project, dream, or mission without one ever again. The word "coach" comes from a town called Kocs in Hungary. Back in 1556, the people of Kocs began to make large carriages that would take people from wherever they were to where they wanted to go. This large carriage was the beginning of what we know as the stagecoach.

A personal coach is like a stagecoach. The primary aim of the coach is to help the leader get from where they are to wherever they want to be. Helping the leader make this trip successfully is the only agenda of the coach, and their success depends on their ability to close this gap.

COMMITMENT # 5: EXPAND YOUR PERSPECTIVE

Without a coach in one's life, leaders can experience:

- Lack of Accountability
- Lack of Focus
- Lack of Direction
- Lack of Perspective
- Lack of Systems
- Lack of Balance

These symptoms can often lead to an ordinary life producing ordinary results in the life and work of a leader. Complacency in a leader's life can also set in after a certain level of success has been accomplished because of general resistance to change. This leads to the leader never breaking out of the achievements of yesterday.

A coach can help challenge a leader to break out of this rut by bringing their dream(s) back into view, keeping them in focus. Leaders are constantly challenged by the elements around them, and it becomes tiring to continue to climb the mountain of success. Extraordinary coaches understand this and know where to go to help the leader dig deep within to bring out the courage to continue the journey to excellence.

Often, we think of a coach as someone who works face-to-face to inspire an individual or team to win a championship. This is just one example. Coaching can come in a variety of forms, including:

- A personal or professional growth book, video, podcast, or audio program
- Interactive websites, blogs, or other virtual resources
- Live training courses or workshops
- A mentor or accountability partner
- A mastermind group of individuals who challenge and coach one another
- A personal coach who works with you one-on-one

COMMITMENT # 5: EXPAND YOUR PERSPECTIVE

Where do you feel you could benefit the most from coaching right now (or in the future)? (Check all the boxes below that apply)

- [ ] Accountability
- [ ] Assistance with clarifying/prioritizing goals
- [ ] Mentorship
- [ ] Focus
- [ ] Planning
- [ ] Strategies to achieve your goals
- [ ] Motivation
- [ ] Encouragement/Guidance

How much focused time are you spending each day/week on personal and professional growth activities? (i.e. reading, watching videos/webinars, listening to audio programs and/or attending events?)

What area of your life do you feel you have the greatest opportunity for improvement to live a more Extraordinary Life?

What are the questions you need to be asked to keep you more accountable to your realizing your dreams and accomplishing your goals?

What will you commit to reading, watching, attending and/or listening to regularly to grow your motivation, mindset, skills and activity level?

Who are the people (mentor, accountability buddy, coach or other person) you will share your goals and/or challenges with and who will hold you to your word? (list their names below)

"THE UNEXAMINED LIFE IS NOT WORTH LIVING."

- SOCRATES

COMMITMENT # 6: RESOLVE TO ACHIEVE YOUR GOALS!

TO LIVE THE EXTRAORDINARY LIFE, WE MUST RESOLVE TO ACHIEVE OUR GOALS AND MEASURE OUR PROGRESS!

WHAT GETS MEASURED GETS DONE

Here is my favorite model for success:

The more you learn... the more you can become...

The more you become... the more you can MEASURABLY achieve...

The more you achieve... the more you can learn...

The more you learn... the more you can become... (This model repeats continuously!)

By taking time to reflect on your plan, progress, and accomplishments, you will learn more about what you are truly capable of achieving with the time, talents, skills, and abilities you have been given. Do not let another month, week or day go by without measuring your success. By determining what you are achieving, you will maintain focus, balance, and direction in your life.

Just as a home builder reviews the construction plan frequently to make sure he is hitting the mark, you must take time once a month or so to check what you are achieving in your life. Find out what is working, so you can ramp that up! If you are not making any progress in accomplishing your action plan, find out why and do whatever it takes to resolve the problem sooner than later.

Measuring the outcomes you generate is where many people start losing steam on their journey to success. That is a shame because knowing what you are measuring and how often you want to measure it is a great way to motivate yourself!

COMMITMENT # 6: RESOLVE TO ACHIEVE YOUR GOALS!

HERE'S WHAT WE WANT TO MEASURE

- Our dreams – Are they clearly defined? Are they really ours or someone else's?
- Our action plans – Do we have a clear plan of action with attainable goals and specific action steps to take?
- Our progress – Are we seeing measurable progress on the plans we've established? Are we headed in the right direction?
- Our use of time – Are we squandering valuable time on activities unrelated to our goals and dreams?

HERE'S HOW OFTEN WE SHOULD MEASURE

- End of the day – Did we do what we needed to do?
- End of the week – Was our week productive?
- End of the month – Were our monthly goals accomplished?
- End of the quarter – Are there achievements to celebrate?
- End of the year – Was the past year successful? How do we know? And by the way, what is the reward?

By measuring our growth and development, we can re-energize, re-vitalize and re-focus ourselves on what matters most right now. The dates I plan to review and measure my progress are...

☐ January	☐ April	☐ July	☐ October
☐ February	☐ May	☐ August	☐ November
☐ March	☐ June	☐ September	☐ December

SUMMARY

Extraordinary Commitment #1 - Will You Live Your Calling? The ringing sound you're hearing regarding the accomplishment of your dreams will not stop. We need more extraordinary leaders like you so we can benefit from your achievements.

Extraordinary Commitment #2 - Will You Engage in Your Dreams? It will take time to discover the dream(s) that act as a catalyst in your life. Finding this agent that accelerates positive change is going to take some trial and error. You must sift through the different thoughts, dreams and ideas and find those you know you've been called to act upon. It's your ultimate purpose in life to fulfill the dreams you've been given.

Extraordinary Commitment #3 - Will You Agree to Make Hard Choices? Every day that passes brings you one day closer to the end of your life. It is the nature of time to run out, and you will find as you age, time will move even faster than it does now. There's no time like today to start living an extraordinary life. Will you choose to start living as if each day were a precious jewel, destined to vanish forever in just twenty-four hours? The choice is up to you!

Extraordinary Commitment #4 - Will You Decide to Fail Forward? You will undoubtedly face many obstacles on your journey. But will you keep pressing on regardless of the challenges you encounter? Will you make The commitment required of all practical dreamers? Will you stay the course and follow your dreams?

Extraordinary Commitment #5 - Will You Expand Your Perspective? The most accomplished leaders know they can't do it alone. They get ideas and support from the very best experts and coaches. So become a serious player in the game of life and follow their example. Be both humble and assertive in pursuing your goal, and when you are ready to be coached, the coach will appear.

Extraordinary Commitment #6 - Will you Resolve to Achieve Your Goals? Taking the Extraordinary Life Challenge will be the most difficult part of your journey. It's where the heavy lifting and hard work is done but it's also where extraordinary leaders are born and developed. Most ordinary people will skip this step and make excuses for why they don't need it or simply procrastinate the opportunity away. Be extraordinary and take this critical step!

FOR MORE RESOURCES VISIT THEEXTRAORDINARYLIFE.COM

EXTRAORDINARY LIFE PLANNER

MY EXTRAORDINARY DAY PLANNER

M T W TH F SA SU --- JAN. FEB. MAR. APR. MAY JUN. JUL. AUG. SEPT. OCT. NOV. DEC.

1 2 3 4 5 6 7 8 9 10 11 12 13 14 15 16 17 18 19 20 21 22 23 24 25 26 27 28 29 30 31

MY TOP 4 EXTRAORDINARY PRIORITIES

- [ ]
- [ ]
- [ ]
- [ ]

EXTRAORDINARY PEOPLE

- [ ]
- [ ]
- [ ]
- [ ]
- [ ]
- [ ]
- [ ]
- [ ]
- [ ]
- [ ]

MY EXTRAORDINARY TASKS

- [ ]
- [ ]
- [ ]
- [ ]

MY EXTRAORDINARY PROJECTS

- [ ]
- [ ]
- [ ]
- [ ]

MY EXTRAORDINARY HABITS

- [ ]
- [ ]
- [ ]
- [ ]

MY EXTRAORDINARY APPOINTMENTS

5:00 ____
5:30 ____
6:00 ____
6:30 ____
7:00 ____
7:30 ____
8:00 ____
8:30 ____
9:00 ____
9:30 ____
10:00 ____
10:30 ____
11:00 ____
11:30 ____
12:00 ____
12:30 ____
1:00 ____
1:30 ____
2:00 ____
2:30 ____

3:00 ____
3:30 ____
4:00 ____
4:30 ____
5:00 ____
5:30 ____
6:00 ____
6:30 ____
7:00 ____
7:30 ____
8:00 ____
8:30 ____
9:00 ____
9:30 ____
10:00 ____
10:30 ____
11:00 ____
11:30 ____
12:00 ____
12:30 ____

MY EXTRAORDINARY NOTES

MY EXTRAORDINARY DAY PLANNER

M T W TH F SA SU --- JAN. FEB. MAR. APR. MAY JUN. JUL. AUG. SEPT. OCT. NOV. DEC.

1 2 3 4 5 6 7 8 9 10 11 12 13 14 15 16 17 18 19 20 21 22 23 24 25 26 27 28 29 30 31

MY TOP 4 EXTRAORDINARY PRIORITIES

☐
☐
☐
☐

EXTRAORDINARY PEOPLE

☐
☐
☐
☐
☐
☐
☐
☐
☐
☐

MY EXTRAORDINARY TASKS

☐
☐
☐
☐

MY EXTRAORDINARY PROJECTS

☐
☐
☐
☐

MY EXTRAORDINARY HABITS

☐
☐
☐
☐

MY EXTRAORDINARY APPOINTMENTS

5:00 ______
5:30 ______
6:00 ______
6:30 ______
7:00 ______
7:30 ______
8:00 ______
8:30 ______
9:00 ______
9:30 ______
10:00 ______
10:30 ______
11:00 ______
11:30 ______
12:00 ______
12:30 ______
1:00 ______
1:30 ______
2:00 ______
2:30 ______

3:00 ______
3:30 ______
4:00 ______
4:30 ______
5:00 ______
5:30 ______
6:00 ______
6:30 ______
7:00 ______
7:30 ______
8:00 ______
8:30 ______
9:00 ______
9:30 ______
10:00 ______
10:30 ______
11:00 ______
11:30 ______
12:00 ______
12:30 ______

MY EXTRAORDINARY NOTES

MY EXTRAORDINARY DAY PLANNER

M T W TH F SA SU --- JAN. FEB. MAR. APR. MAY JUN. JUL. AUG. SEPT. OCT. NOV. DEC.

1 2 3 4 5 6 7 8 9 10 11 12 13 14 15 16 17 18 19 20 21 22 23 24 25 26 27 28 29 30 31

MY TOP 4 EXTRAORDINARY PRIORITIES

- [ ]
- [ ]
- [ ]
- [ ]

EXTRAORDINARY PEOPLE

- [ ]
- [ ]
- [ ]
- [ ]
- [ ]
- [ ]
- [ ]
- [ ]
- [ ]
- [ ]

MY EXTRAORDINARY TASKS

- [ ]
- [ ]
- [ ]
- [ ]

MY EXTRAORDINARY PROJECTS

- [ ]
- [ ]
- [ ]
- [ ]

MY EXTRAORDINARY HABITS

- [ ]
- [ ]
- [ ]
- [ ]

MY EXTRAORDINARY APPOINTMENTS

5:00 ______
5:30 ______
6:00 ______
6:30 ______
7:00 ______
7:30 ______
8:00 ______
8:30 ______
9:00 ______
9:30 ______
10:00 ______
10:30 ______
11:00 ______
11:30 ______
12:00 ______
12:30 ______
1:00 ______
1:30 ______
2:00 ______
2:30 ______

3:00 ______
3:30 ______
4:00 ______
4:30 ______
5:00 ______
5:30 ______
6:00 ______
6:30 ______
7:00 ______
7:30 ______
8:00 ______
8:30 ______
9:00 ______
9:30 ______
10:00 ______
10:30 ______
11:00 ______
11:30 ______
12:00 ______
12:30 ______

MY EXTRAORDINARY NOTES

MY EXTRAORDINARY DAY PLANNER

M T W TH F SA SU --- JAN. FEB. MAR. APR. MAY JUN. JUL. AUG. SEPT. OCT. NOV. DEC.

1 2 3 4 5 6 7 8 9 10 11 12 13 14 15 16 17 18 19 20 21 22 23 24 25 26 27 28 29 30 31

MY TOP 4 EXTRAORDINARY PRIORITIES

- [ ]
- [ ]
- [ ]
- [ ]

MY EXTRAORDINARY PROJECTS

- [ ]
- [ ]
- [ ]
- [ ]

EXTRAORDINARY PEOPLE

- [ ]
- [ ]
- [ ]
- [ ]
- [ ]
- [ ]
- [ ]
- [ ]
- [ ]
- [ ]

MY EXTRAORDINARY TASKS

- [ ]
- [ ]
- [ ]
- [ ]

MY EXTRAORDINARY HABITS

- [ ]
- [ ]
- [ ]
- [ ]

MY EXTRAORDINARY APPOINTMENTS

5:00 ____
5:30 ____
6:00 ____
6:30 ____
7:00 ____
7:30 ____
8:00 ____
8:30 ____
9:00 ____
9:30 ____
10:00 ____
10:30 ____
11:00 ____
11:30 ____
12:00 ____
12:30 ____
1:00 ____
1:30 ____
2:00 ____
2:30 ____
3:00 ____
3:30 ____
4:00 ____
4:30 ____
5:00 ____
5:30 ____
6:00 ____
6:30 ____
7:00 ____
7:30 ____
8:00 ____
8:30 ____
9:00 ____
9:30 ____
10:00 ____
10:30 ____
11:00 ____
11:30 ____
12:00 ____
12:30 ____

MY EXTRAORDINARY NOTES

MY EXTRAORDINARY DAY PLANNER

M T W TH F SA SU --- JAN. FEB. MAR. APR. MAY JUN. JUL. AUG. SEPT. OCT. NOV. DEC.

1 2 3 4 5 6 7 8 9 10 11 12 13 14 15 16 17 18 19 20 21 22 23 24 25 26 27 28 29 30 31

MY TOP 4 EXTRAORDINARY PRIORITIES

- [ ]
- [ ]
- [ ]
- [ ]

MY EXTRAORDINARY PROJECTS

- [ ]
- [ ]
- [ ]
- [ ]

EXTRAORDINARY PEOPLE

- [ ]
- [ ]
- [ ]
- [ ]
- [ ]
- [ ]
- [ ]
- [ ]
- [ ]
- [ ]

MY EXTRAORDINARY TASKS

- [ ]
- [ ]
- [ ]
- [ ]

MY EXTRAORDINARY HABITS

- [ ]
- [ ]
- [ ]
- [ ]

MY EXTRAORDINARY APPOINTMENTS

5:00		3:00	
5:30		3:30	
6:00		4:00	
6:30		4:30	
7:00		5:00	
7:30		5:30	
8:00		6:00	
8:30		6:30	
9:00		7:00	
9:30		7:30	
10:00		8:00	
10:30		8:30	
11:00		9:00	
11:30		9:30	
12:00		10:00	
12:30		10:30	
1:00		11:00	
1:30		11:30	
2:00		12:00	
2:30		12:30	

MY EXTRAORDINARY NOTES

MY EXTRAORDINARY DAY PLANNER

M T W TH F SA SU --- JAN. FEB. MAR. APR. MAY JUN. JUL. AUG. SEPT. OCT. NOV. DEC.

1 2 3 4 5 6 7 8 9 10 11 12 13 14 15 16 17 18 19 20 21 22 23 24 25 26 27 28 29 30 31

MY TOP 4 EXTRAORDINARY PRIORITIES

- [ ]
- [ ]
- [ ]
- [ ]

EXTRAORDINARY PEOPLE

- [ ]
- [ ]
- [ ]
- [ ]
- [ ]
- [ ]
- [ ]
- [ ]
- [ ]
- [ ]

MY EXTRAORDINARY TASKS

- [ ]
- [ ]
- [ ]
- [ ]

MY EXTRAORDINARY PROJECTS

- [ ]
- [ ]
- [ ]
- [ ]

MY EXTRAORDINARY HABITS

- [ ]
- [ ]
- [ ]
- [ ]

MY EXTRAORDINARY APPOINTMENTS

5:00 __________
5:30 __________
6:00 __________
6:30 __________
7:00 __________
7:30 __________
8:00 __________
8:30 __________
9:00 __________
9:30 __________
10:00 __________
10:30 __________
11:00 __________
11:30 __________
12:00 __________
12:30 __________
1:00 __________
1:30 __________
2:00 __________
2:30 __________
3:00 __________
3:30 __________
4:00 __________
4:30 __________
5:00 __________
5:30 __________
6:00 __________
6:30 __________
7:00 __________
7:30 __________
8:00 __________
8:30 __________
9:00 __________
9:30 __________
10:00 __________
10:30 __________
11:00 __________
11:30 __________
12:00 __________
12:30 __________

MY EXTRAORDINARY NOTES

MY EXTRAORDINARY DAY PLANNER

M T W TH F SA SU --- JAN. FEB. MAR. APR. MAY JUN. JUL. AUG. SEPT. OCT. NOV. DEC.

1 2 3 4 5 6 7 8 9 10 11 12 13 14 15 16 17 18 19 20 21 22 23 24 25 26 27 28 29 30 31

MY TOP 4 EXTRAORDINARY PRIORITIES

- [ ]
- [ ]
- [ ]
- [ ]

MY EXTRAORDINARY PROJECTS

- [ ]
- [ ]
- [ ]
- [ ]

EXTRAORDINARY PEOPLE

- [ ]
- [ ]
- [ ]
- [ ]
- [ ]
- [ ]
- [ ]
- [ ]
- [ ]
- [ ]

MY EXTRAORDINARY TASKS

- [ ]
- [ ]
- [ ]
- [ ]

MY EXTRAORDINARY HABITS

- [ ]
- [ ]
- [ ]
- [ ]

MY EXTRAORDINARY APPOINTMENTS

5:00 ______

5:30 ______

6:00 ______

6:30 ______

7:00 ______

7:30 ______

8:00 ______

8:30 ______

9:00 ______

9:30 ______

10:00 ______

10:30 ______

11:00 ______

11:30 ______

12:00 ______

12:30 ______

1:00 ______

1:30 ______

2:00 ______

2:30 ______

3:00 ______

3:30 ______

4:00 ______

4:30 ______

5:00 ______

5:30 ______

6:00 ______

6:30 ______

7:00 ______

7:30 ______

8:00 ______

8:30 ______

9:00 ______

9:30 ______

10:00 ______

10:30 ______

11:00 ______

11:30 ______

12:00 ______

12:30 ______

MY EXTRAORDINARY NOTES

MY EXTRAORDINARY DAY PLANNER

M T W TH F SA SU --- JAN. FEB. MAR. APR. MAY JUN. JUL. AUG. SEPT. OCT. NOV. DEC.

1 2 3 4 5 6 7 8 9 10 11 12 13 14 15 16 17 18 19 20 21 22 23 24 25 26 27 28 29 30 31

MY TOP 4 EXTRAORDINARY PRIORITIES

- [ ]
- [ ]
- [ ]
- [ ]

EXTRAORDINARY PEOPLE

- [ ]
- [ ]
- [ ]
- [ ]
- [ ]
- [ ]
- [ ]
- [ ]
- [ ]
- [ ]

MY EXTRAORDINARY TASKS

- [ ]
- [ ]
- [ ]
- [ ]

MY EXTRAORDINARY PROJECTS

- [ ]
- [ ]
- [ ]
- [ ]

MY EXTRAORDINARY HABITS

- [ ]
- [ ]
- [ ]
- [ ]

MY EXTRAORDINARY APPOINTMENTS

5:00 ______

5:30 ______

6:00 ______

6:30 ______

7:00 ______

7:30 ______

8:00 ______

8:30 ______

9:00 ______

9:30 ______

10:00 ______

10:30 ______

11:00 ______

11:30 ______

12:00 ______

12:30 ______

1:00 ______

1:30 ______

2:00 ______

2:30 ______

3:00 ______

3:30 ______

4:00 ______

4:30 ______

5:00 ______

5:30 ______

6:00 ______

6:30 ______

7:00 ______

7:30 ______

8:00 ______

8:30 ______

9:00 ______

9:30 ______

10:00 ______

10:30 ______

11:00 ______

11:30 ______

12:00 ______

12:30 ______

MY EXTRAORDINARY NOTES

MY EXTRAORDINARY DAY PLANNER

M T W TH F SA SU --- JAN. FEB. MAR. APR. MAY JUN. JUL. AUG. SEPT. OCT. NOV. DEC.

1 2 3 4 5 6 7 8 9 10 11 12 13 14 15 16 17 18 19 20 21 22 23 24 25 26 27 28 29 30 31

MY TOP 4 EXTRAORDINARY PRIORITIES

- [ ]
- [ ]
- [ ]
- [ ]

EXTRAORDINARY PEOPLE

- [ ]
- [ ]
- [ ]
- [ ]
- [ ]
- [ ]
- [ ]
- [ ]
- [ ]
- [ ]

MY EXTRAORDINARY TASKS

- [ ]
- [ ]
- [ ]
- [ ]

MY EXTRAORDINARY PROJECTS

- [ ]
- [ ]
- [ ]
- [ ]

MY EXTRAORDINARY HABITS

- [ ]
- [ ]
- [ ]
- [ ]

MY EXTRAORDINARY APPOINTMENTS

5:00		3:00	
5:30		3:30	
6:00		4:00	
6:30		4:30	
7:00		5:00	
7:30		5:30	
8:00		6:00	
8:30		6:30	
9:00		7:00	
9:30		7:30	
10:00		8:00	
10:30		8:30	
11:00		9:00	
11:30		9:30	
12:00		10:00	
12:30		10:30	
1:00		11:00	
1:30		11:30	
2:00		12:00	
2:30		12:30	

MY EXTRAORDINARY NOTES

MY EXTRAORDINARY DAY PLANNER

M T W TH F SA SU --- JAN. FEB. MAR. APR. MAY JUN. JUL. AUG. SEPT. OCT. NOV. DEC.

1 2 3 4 5 6 7 8 9 10 11 12 13 14 15 16 17 18 19 20 21 22 23 24 25 26 27 28 29 30 31

MY TOP 4 EXTRAORDINARY PRIORITIES

- [ ]
- [ ]
- [ ]
- [ ]

MY EXTRAORDINARY PROJECTS

- [ ]
- [ ]
- [ ]
- [ ]

EXTRAORDINARY PEOPLE

- [ ]
- [ ]
- [ ]
- [ ]
- [ ]
- [ ]
- [ ]
- [ ]
- [ ]
- [ ]

MY EXTRAORDINARY TASKS

- [ ]
- [ ]
- [ ]
- [ ]

MY EXTRAORDINARY HABITS

- [ ]
- [ ]
- [ ]
- [ ]

MY EXTRAORDINARY APPOINTMENTS

5:00		3:00	
5:30		3:30	
6:00		4:00	
6:30		4:30	
7:00		5:00	
7:30		5:30	
8:00		6:00	
8:30		6:30	
9:00		7:00	
9:30		7:30	
10:00		8:00	
10:30		8:30	
11:00		9:00	
11:30		9:30	
12:00		10:00	
12:30		10:30	
1:00		11:00	
1:30		11:30	
2:00		12:00	
2:30		12:30	

MY EXTRAORDINARY NOTES

MY EXTRAORDINARY DAY PLANNER

M T W TH F SA SU --- JAN. FEB. MAR. APR. MAY JUN. JUL. AUG. SEPT. OCT. NOV. DEC.

1 2 3 4 5 6 7 8 9 10 11 12 13 14 15 16 17 18 19 20 21 22 23 24 25 26 27 28 29 30 31

MY TOP 4 EXTRAORDINARY PRIORITIES

- ☐
- ☐
- ☐
- ☐

EXTRAORDINARY PEOPLE

- ☐
- ☐
- ☐
- ☐
- ☐
- ☐
- ☐
- ☐
- ☐
- ☐

MY EXTRAORDINARY TASKS

- ☐
- ☐
- ☐
- ☐

MY EXTRAORDINARY PROJECTS

- ☐
- ☐
- ☐
- ☐

MY EXTRAORDINARY HABITS

- ☐
- ☐
- ☐
- ☐

MY EXTRAORDINARY APPOINTMENTS

5:00 ____
5:30 ____
6:00 ____
6:30 ____
7:00 ____
7:30 ____
8:00 ____
8:30 ____
9:00 ____
9:30 ____
10:00 ____
10:30 ____
11:00 ____
11:30 ____
12:00 ____
12:30 ____
1:00 ____
1:30 ____
2:00 ____
2:30 ____

3:00 ____
3:30 ____
4:00 ____
4:30 ____
5:00 ____
5:30 ____
6:00 ____
6:30 ____
7:00 ____
7:30 ____
8:00 ____
8:30 ____
9:00 ____
9:30 ____
10:00 ____
10:30 ____
11:00 ____
11:30 ____
12:00 ____
12:30 ____

MY EXTRAORDINARY NOTES

MY EXTRAORDINARY DAY PLANNER

M T W TH F SA SU --- JAN. FEB. MAR. APR. MAY JUN. JUL. AUG. SEPT. OCT. NOV. DEC.

1 2 3 4 5 6 7 8 9 10 11 12 13 14 15 16 17 18 19 20 21 22 23 24 25 26 27 28 29 30 31

MY TOP 4 EXTRAORDINARY PRIORITIES

- [ ]
- [ ]
- [ ]
- [ ]

MY EXTRAORDINARY PROJECTS

- [ ]
- [ ]
- [ ]
- [ ]

EXTRAORDINARY PEOPLE

- [ ]
- [ ]
- [ ]
- [ ]
- [ ]
- [ ]
- [ ]
- [ ]
- [ ]
- [ ]

MY EXTRAORDINARY TASKS

- [ ]
- [ ]
- [ ]
- [ ]

MY EXTRAORDINARY HABITS

- [ ]
- [ ]
- [ ]
- [ ]

MY EXTRAORDINARY APPOINTMENTS

5:00 ______
5:30 ______
6:00 ______
6:30 ______
7:00 ______
7:30 ______
8:00 ______
8:30 ______
9:00 ______
9:30 ______
10:00 ______
10:30 ______
11:00 ______
11:30 ______
12:00 ______
12:30 ______
1:00 ______
1:30 ______
2:00 ______
2:30 ______

3:00 ______
3:30 ______
4:00 ______
4:30 ______
5:00 ______
5:30 ______
6:00 ______
6:30 ______
7:00 ______
7:30 ______
8:00 ______
8:30 ______
9:00 ______
9:30 ______
10:00 ______
10:30 ______
11:00 ______
11:30 ______
12:00 ______
12:30 ______

MY EXTRAORDINARY NOTES

MY EXTRAORDINARY DAY PLANNER

M T W TH F SA SU --- JAN. FEB. MAR. APR. MAY JUN. JUL. AUG. SEPT. OCT. NOV. DEC.

1 2 3 4 5 6 7 8 9 10 11 12 13 14 15 16 17 18 19 20 21 22 23 24 25 26 27 28 29 30 31

MY TOP 4 EXTRAORDINARY PRIORITIES

- [ ]
- [ ]
- [ ]
- [ ]

EXTRAORDINARY PEOPLE

- [ ]
- [ ]
- [ ]
- [ ]
- [ ]
- [ ]
- [ ]
- [ ]
- [ ]
- [ ]

MY EXTRAORDINARY TASKS

- [ ]
- [ ]
- [ ]
- [ ]

MY EXTRAORDINARY PROJECTS

- [ ]
- [ ]
- [ ]
- [ ]

MY EXTRAORDINARY HABITS

- [ ]
- [ ]
- [ ]
- [ ]

MY EXTRAORDINARY APPOINTMENTS

5:00 ____________
5:30 ____________
6:00 ____________
6:30 ____________
7:00 ____________
7:30 ____________
8:00 ____________
8:30 ____________
9:00 ____________
9:30 ____________
10:00 ____________
10:30 ____________
11:00 ____________
11:30 ____________
12:00 ____________
12:30 ____________
1:00 ____________
1:30 ____________
2:00 ____________
2:30 ____________
3:00 ____________
3:30 ____________
4:00 ____________
4:30 ____________
5:00 ____________
5:30 ____________
6:00 ____________
6:30 ____________
7:00 ____________
7:30 ____________
8:00 ____________
8:30 ____________
9:00 ____________
9:30 ____________
10:00 ____________
10:30 ____________
11:00 ____________
11:30 ____________
12:00 ____________
12:30 ____________

MY EXTRAORDINARY NOTES

MY EXTRAORDINARY DAY PLANNER

M T W TH F SA SU --- JAN. FEB. MAR. APR. MAY JUN. JUL. AUG. SEPT. OCT. NOV. DEC.

1 2 3 4 5 6 7 8 9 10 11 12 13 14 15 16 17 18 19 20 21 22 23 24 25 26 27 28 29 30 31

MY TOP 4 EXTRAORDINARY PRIORITIES

- [ ]
- [ ]
- [ ]
- [ ]

MY EXTRAORDINARY PROJECTS

- [ ]
- [ ]
- [ ]
- [ ]

EXTRAORDINARY PEOPLE

- [ ]
- [ ]
- [ ]
- [ ]
- [ ]
- [ ]
- [ ]
- [ ]
- [ ]
- [ ]

MY EXTRAORDINARY TASKS

- [ ]
- [ ]
- [ ]
- [ ]

MY EXTRAORDINARY HABITS

- [ ]
- [ ]
- [ ]
- [ ]

MY EXTRAORDINARY APPOINTMENTS

5:00 ____
5:30 ____
6:00 ____
6:30 ____
7:00 ____
7:30 ____
8:00 ____
8:30 ____
9:00 ____
9:30 ____
10:00 ____
10:30 ____
11:00 ____
11:30 ____
12:00 ____
12:30 ____
1:00 ____
1:30 ____
2:00 ____
2:30 ____
3:00 ____
3:30 ____
4:00 ____
4:30 ____
5:00 ____
5:30 ____
6:00 ____
6:30 ____
7:00 ____
7:30 ____
8:00 ____
8:30 ____
9:00 ____
9:30 ____
10:00 ____
10:30 ____
11:00 ____
11:30 ____
12:00 ____
12:30 ____

MY EXTRAORDINARY NOTES

MY EXTRAORDINARY DAY PLANNER

M T W TH F SA SU --- JAN. FEB. MAR. APR. MAY JUN. JUL. AUG. SEPT. OCT. NOV. DEC.

1 2 3 4 5 6 7 8 9 10 11 12 13 14 15 16 17 18 19 20 21 22 23 24 25 26 27 28 29 30 31

MY TOP 4 EXTRAORDINARY PRIORITIES

- [ ]
- [ ]
- [ ]
- [ ]

EXTRAORDINARY PEOPLE

- [ ]
- [ ]
- [ ]
- [ ]
- [ ]
- [ ]
- [ ]
- [ ]
- [ ]
- [ ]

MY EXTRAORDINARY TASKS

- [ ]
- [ ]
- [ ]
- [ ]

MY EXTRAORDINARY PROJECTS

- [ ]
- [ ]
- [ ]
- [ ]

MY EXTRAORDINARY HABITS

- [ ]
- [ ]
- [ ]
- [ ]

MY EXTRAORDINARY APPOINTMENTS

5:00 __________
5:30 __________
6:00 __________
6:30 __________
7:00 __________
7:30 __________
8:00 __________
8:30 __________
9:00 __________
9:30 __________
10:00 __________
10:30 __________
11:00 __________
11:30 __________
12:00 __________
12:30 __________
1:00 __________
1:30 __________
2:00 __________
2:30 __________
3:00 __________
3:30 __________
4:00 __________
4:30 __________
5:00 __________
5:30 __________
6:00 __________
6:30 __________
7:00 __________
7:30 __________
8:00 __________
8:30 __________
9:00 __________
9:30 __________
10:00 __________
10:30 __________
11:00 __________
11:30 __________
12:00 __________
12:30 __________

MY EXTRAORDINARY NOTES

MY EXTRAORDINARY DAY PLANNER

M T W TH F SA SU --- JAN. FEB. MAR. APR. MAY JUN. JUL. AUG. SEPT. OCT. NOV. DEC.

1 2 3 4 5 6 7 8 9 10 11 12 13 14 15 16 17 18 19 20 21 22 23 24 25 26 27 28 29 30 31

MY TOP 4 EXTRAORDINARY PRIORITIES

- [ ]
- [ ]
- [ ]
- [ ]

EXTRAORDINARY PEOPLE

- [ ]
- [ ]
- [ ]
- [ ]
- [ ]
- [ ]
- [ ]
- [ ]
- [ ]
- [ ]

MY EXTRAORDINARY TASKS

- [ ]
- [ ]
- [ ]
- [ ]

MY EXTRAORDINARY PROJECTS

- [ ]
- [ ]
- [ ]
- [ ]

MY EXTRAORDINARY HABITS

- [ ]
- [ ]
- [ ]
- [ ]

MY EXTRAORDINARY APPOINTMENTS

5:00 ______
5:30 ______
6:00 ______
6:30 ______
7:00 ______
7:30 ______
8:00 ______
8:30 ______
9:00 ______
9:30 ______
10:00 ______
10:30 ______
11:00 ______
11:30 ______
12:00 ______
12:30 ______
1:00 ______
1:30 ______
2:00 ______
2:30 ______

3:00 ______
3:30 ______
4:00 ______
4:30 ______
5:00 ______
5:30 ______
6:00 ______
6:30 ______
7:00 ______
7:30 ______
8:00 ______
8:30 ______
9:00 ______
9:30 ______
10:00 ______
10:30 ______
11:00 ______
11:30 ______
12:00 ______
12:30 ______

MY EXTRAORDINARY NOTES

MY EXTRAORDINARY DAY PLANNER

M T W TH F SA SU --- JAN. FEB. MAR. APR. MAY JUN. JUL. AUG. SEPT. OCT. NOV. DEC.

1 2 3 4 5 6 7 8 9 10 11 12 13 14 15 16 17 18 19 20 21 22 23 24 25 26 27 28 29 30 31

MY TOP 4 EXTRAORDINARY PRIORITIES

- [ ]
- [ ]
- [ ]
- [ ]

MY EXTRAORDINARY PROJECTS

- [ ]
- [ ]
- [ ]
- [ ]

EXTRAORDINARY PEOPLE

- [ ]
- [ ]
- [ ]
- [ ]
- [ ]
- [ ]
- [ ]
- [ ]
- [ ]
- [ ]

MY EXTRAORDINARY TASKS

- [ ]
- [ ]
- [ ]
- [ ]

MY EXTRAORDINARY HABITS

- [ ]
- [ ]
- [ ]
- [ ]

MY EXTRAORDINARY APPOINTMENTS

5:00 _____
5:30 _____
6:00 _____
6:30 _____
7:00 _____
7:30 _____
8:00 _____
8:30 _____
9:00 _____
9:30 _____
10:00 _____
10:30 _____
11:00 _____
11:30 _____
12:00 _____
12:30 _____
1:00 _____
1:30 _____
2:00 _____
2:30 _____
3:00 _____
3:30 _____
4:00 _____
4:30 _____
5:00 _____
5:30 _____
6:00 _____
6:30 _____
7:00 _____
7:30 _____
8:00 _____
8:30 _____
9:00 _____
9:30 _____
10:00 _____
10:30 _____
11:00 _____
11:30 _____
12:00 _____
12:30 _____

MY EXTRAORDINARY NOTES

MY EXTRAORDINARY DAY PLANNER

M T W TH F SA SU --- JAN. FEB. MAR. APR. MAY JUN. JUL. AUG. SEPT. OCT. NOV. DEC.

1 2 3 4 5 6 7 8 9 10 11 12 13 14 15 16 17 18 19 20 21 22 23 24 25 26 27 28 29 30 31

MY TOP 4 EXTRAORDINARY PRIORITIES

- [ ]
- [ ]
- [ ]
- [ ]

EXTRAORDINARY PEOPLE

- [ ]
- [ ]
- [ ]
- [ ]
- [ ]
- [ ]
- [ ]
- [ ]
- [ ]
- [ ]

MY EXTRAORDINARY TASKS

- [ ]
- [ ]
- [ ]
- [ ]

MY EXTRAORDINARY PROJECTS

- [ ]
- [ ]
- [ ]
- [ ]

MY EXTRAORDINARY HABITS

- [ ]
- [ ]
- [ ]
- [ ]

MY EXTRAORDINARY APPOINTMENTS

5:00 ______
5:30 ______
6:00 ______
6:30 ______
7:00 ______
7:30 ______
8:00 ______
8:30 ______
9:00 ______
9:30 ______
10:00 ______
10:30 ______
11:00 ______
11:30 ______
12:00 ______
12:30 ______
1:00 ______
1:30 ______
2:00 ______
2:30 ______
3:00 ______
3:30 ______
4:00 ______
4:30 ______
5:00 ______
5:30 ______
6:00 ______
6:30 ______
7:00 ______
7:30 ______
8:00 ______
8:30 ______
9:00 ______
9:30 ______
10:00 ______
10:30 ______
11:00 ______
11:30 ______
12:00 ______
12:30 ______

MY EXTRAORDINARY NOTES

MY EXTRAORDINARY DAY PLANNER

M T W TH F SA SU --- JAN. FEB. MAR. APR. MAY JUN. JUL. AUG. SEPT. OCT. NOV. DEC.

1 2 3 4 5 6 7 8 9 10 11 12 13 14 15 16 17 18 19 20 21 22 23 24 25 26 27 28 29 30 31

MY TOP 4 EXTRAORDINARY PRIORITIES

- [ ]
- [ ]
- [ ]
- [ ]

EXTRAORDINARY PEOPLE

- [ ]
- [ ]
- [ ]
- [ ]
- [ ]
- [ ]
- [ ]
- [ ]
- [ ]
- [ ]

MY EXTRAORDINARY TASKS

- [ ]
- [ ]
- [ ]
- [ ]

MY EXTRAORDINARY PROJECTS

- [ ]
- [ ]
- [ ]
- [ ]

MY EXTRAORDINARY HABITS

- [ ]
- [ ]
- [ ]
- [ ]

MY EXTRAORDINARY APPOINTMENTS

5:00		3:00	
5:30		3:30	
6:00		4:00	
6:30		4:30	
7:00		5:00	
7:30		5:30	
8:00		6:00	
8:30		6:30	
9:00		7:00	
9:30		7:30	
10:00		8:00	
10:30		8:30	
11:00		9:00	
11:30		9:30	
12:00		10:00	
12:30		10:30	
1:00		11:00	
1:30		11:30	
2:00		12:00	
2:30		12:30	

MY EXTRAORDINARY NOTES

MY EXTRAORDINARY DAY PLANNER

M T W TH F SA SU --- JAN. FEB. MAR. APR. MAY JUN. JUL. AUG. SEPT. OCT. NOV. DEC.

1 2 3 4 5 6 7 8 9 10 11 12 13 14 15 16 17 18 19 20 21 22 23 24 25 26 27 28 29 30 31

MY TOP 4 EXTRAORDINARY PRIORITIES

- [ ]
- [ ]
- [ ]
- [ ]

MY EXTRAORDINARY PROJECTS

- [ ]
- [ ]
- [ ]
- [ ]

EXTRAORDINARY PEOPLE

- [ ]
- [ ]
- [ ]
- [ ]
- [ ]
- [ ]
- [ ]
- [ ]
- [ ]
- [ ]

MY EXTRAORDINARY TASKS

- [ ]
- [ ]
- [ ]
- [ ]

MY EXTRAORDINARY HABITS

- [ ]
- [ ]
- [ ]
- [ ]

MY EXTRAORDINARY APPOINTMENTS

5:00 ____
5:30 ____
6:00 ____
6:30 ____
7:00 ____
7:30 ____
8:00 ____
8:30 ____
9:00 ____
9:30 ____
10:00 ____
10:30 ____
11:00 ____
11:30 ____
12:00 ____
12:30 ____
1:00 ____
1:30 ____
2:00 ____
2:30 ____

3:00 ____
3:30 ____
4:00 ____
4:30 ____
5:00 ____
5:30 ____
6:00 ____
6:30 ____
7:00 ____
7:30 ____
8:00 ____
8:30 ____
9:00 ____
9:30 ____
10:00 ____
10:30 ____
11:00 ____
11:30 ____
12:00 ____
12:30 ____

MY EXTRAORDINARY NOTES

MY EXTRAORDINARY DAY PLANNER

M T W TH F SA SU --- JAN. FEB. MAR. APR. MAY JUN. JUL. AUG. SEPT. OCT. NOV. DEC.

1 2 3 4 5 6 7 8 9 10 11 12 13 14 15 16 17 18 19 20 21 22 23 24 25 26 27 28 29 30 31

MY TOP 4 EXTRAORDINARY PRIORITIES	EXTRAORDINARY PEOPLE	MY EXTRAORDINARY TASKS
☐ ☐ ☐ ☐	☐ ☐ ☐ ☐ ☐ ☐ ☐ ☐ ☐ ☐	☐ ☐ ☐ ☐
MY EXTRAORDINARY PROJECTS		MY EXTRAORDINARY HABITS
☐ ☐ ☐ ☐		☐ ☐ ☐ ☐

MY EXTRAORDINARY APPOINTMENTS

5:00 ____________	3:00 ____________
5:30 ____________	3:30 ____________
6:00 ____________	4:00 ____________
6:30 ____________	4:30 ____________
7:00 ____________	5:00 ____________
7:30 ____________	5:30 ____________
8:00 ____________	6:00 ____________
8:30 ____________	6:30 ____________
9:00 ____________	7:00 ____________
9:30 ____________	7:30 ____________
10:00 ____________	8:00 ____________
10:30 ____________	8:30 ____________
11:00 ____________	9:00 ____________
11:30 ____________	9:30 ____________
12:00 ____________	10:00 ____________
12:30 ____________	10:30 ____________
1:00 ____________	11:00 ____________
1:30 ____________	11:30 ____________
2:00 ____________	12:00 ____________
2:30 ____________	12:30 ____________

MY EXTRAORDINARY NOTES

MY EXTRAORDINARY DAY PLANNER

M T W TH F SA SU --- JAN. FEB. MAR. APR. MAY JUN. JUL. AUG. SEPT. OCT. NOV. DEC.

1 2 3 4 5 6 7 8 9 10 11 12 13 14 15 16 17 18 19 20 21 22 23 24 25 26 27 28 29 30 31

MY TOP 4 EXTRAORDINARY PRIORITIES

- [ ]
- [ ]
- [ ]
- [ ]

EXTRAORDINARY PEOPLE

- [ ]
- [ ]
- [ ]
- [ ]
- [ ]
- [ ]
- [ ]
- [ ]
- [ ]
- [ ]

MY EXTRAORDINARY TASKS

- [ ]
- [ ]
- [ ]
- [ ]

MY EXTRAORDINARY PROJECTS

- [ ]
- [ ]
- [ ]
- [ ]

MY EXTRAORDINARY HABITS

- [ ]
- [ ]
- [ ]
- [ ]

MY EXTRAORDINARY APPOINTMENTS

5:00	3:00
5:30	3:30
6:00	4:00
6:30	4:30
7:00	5:00
7:30	5:30
8:00	6:00
8:30	6:30
9:00	7:00
9:30	7:30
10:00	8:00
10:30	8:30
11:00	9:00
11:30	9:30
12:00	10:00
12:30	10:30
1:00	11:00
1:30	11:30
2:00	12:00
2:30	12:30

MY EXTRAORDINARY NOTES

MY EXTRAORDINARY DAY PLANNER

M T W TH F SA SU --- JAN. FEB. MAR. APR. MAY JUN. JUL. AUG. SEPT. OCT. NOV. DEC.

1 2 3 4 5 6 7 8 9 10 11 12 13 14 15 16 17 18 19 20 21 22 23 24 25 26 27 28 29 30 31

MY TOP 4 EXTRAORDINARY PRIORITIES

- [ ]
- [ ]
- [ ]
- [ ]

EXTRAORDINARY PEOPLE

- [ ]
- [ ]
- [ ]
- [ ]
- [ ]
- [ ]
- [ ]
- [ ]
- [ ]
- [ ]

MY EXTRAORDINARY TASKS

- [ ]
- [ ]
- [ ]
- [ ]

MY EXTRAORDINARY PROJECTS

- [ ]
- [ ]
- [ ]
- [ ]

MY EXTRAORDINARY HABITS

- [ ]
- [ ]
- [ ]
- [ ]

MY EXTRAORDINARY APPOINTMENTS

5:00		3:00	
5:30		3:30	
6:00		4:00	
6:30		4:30	
7:00		5:00	
7:30		5:30	
8:00		6:00	
8:30		6:30	
9:00		7:00	
9:30		7:30	
10:00		8:00	
10:30		8:30	
11:00		9:00	
11:30		9:30	
12:00		10:00	
12:30		10:30	
1:00		11:00	
1:30		11:30	
2:00		12:00	
2:30		12:30	

MY EXTRAORDINARY NOTES

MY EXTRAORDINARY DAY PLANNER

M T W TH F SA SU --- JAN. FEB. MAR. APR. MAY JUN. JUL. AUG. SEPT. OCT. NOV. DEC.

1 2 3 4 5 6 7 8 9 10 11 12 13 14 15 16 17 18 19 20 21 22 23 24 25 26 27 28 29 30 31

MY TOP 4 EXTRAORDINARY PRIORITIES

- ☐
- ☐
- ☐
- ☐

MY EXTRAORDINARY PROJECTS

- ☐
- ☐
- ☐
- ☐

EXTRAORDINARY PEOPLE

- ☐
- ☐
- ☐
- ☐
- ☐
- ☐
- ☐
- ☐
- ☐
- ☐

MY EXTRAORDINARY TASKS

- ☐
- ☐
- ☐
- ☐

MY EXTRAORDINARY HABITS

- ☐
- ☐
- ☐
- ☐

MY EXTRAORDINARY APPOINTMENTS

5:00 ______
5:30 ______
6:00 ______
6:30 ______
7:00 ______
7:30 ______
8:00 ______
8:30 ______
9:00 ______
9:30 ______
10:00 ______
10:30 ______
11:00 ______
11:30 ______
12:00 ______
12:30 ______
1:00 ______
1:30 ______
2:00 ______
2:30 ______
3:00 ______
3:30 ______
4:00 ______
4:30 ______
5:00 ______
5:30 ______
6:00 ______
6:30 ______
7:00 ______
7:30 ______
8:00 ______
8:30 ______
9:00 ______
9:30 ______
10:00 ______
10:30 ______
11:00 ______
11:30 ______
12:00 ______
12:30 ______

MY EXTRAORDINARY NOTES

MY EXTRAORDINARY DAY PLANNER

M T W TH F SA SU --- JAN. FEB. MAR. APR. MAY JUN. JUL. AUG. SEPT. OCT. NOV. DEC.

1 2 3 4 5 6 7 8 9 10 11 12 13 14 15 16 17 18 19 20 21 22 23 24 25 26 27 28 29 30 31

MY TOP 4 EXTRAORDINARY PRIORITIES

- [ ]
- [ ]
- [ ]
- [ ]

EXTRAORDINARY PEOPLE

- [ ]
- [ ]
- [ ]
- [ ]
- [ ]
- [ ]
- [ ]
- [ ]
- [ ]
- [ ]

MY EXTRAORDINARY TASKS

- [ ]
- [ ]
- [ ]
- [ ]

MY EXTRAORDINARY PROJECTS

- [ ]
- [ ]
- [ ]
- [ ]

MY EXTRAORDINARY HABITS

- [ ]
- [ ]
- [ ]
- [ ]

MY EXTRAORDINARY APPOINTMENTS

5:00 ______

5:30 ______

6:00 ______

6:30 ______

7:00 ______

7:30 ______

8:00 ______

8:30 ______

9:00 ______

9:30 ______

10:00 ______

10:30 ______

11:00 ______

11:30 ______

12:00 ______

12:30 ______

1:00 ______

1:30 ______

2:00 ______

2:30 ______

3:00 ______

3:30 ______

4:00 ______

4:30 ______

5:00 ______

5:30 ______

6:00 ______

6:30 ______

7:00 ______

7:30 ______

8:00 ______

8:30 ______

9:00 ______

9:30 ______

10:00 ______

10:30 ______

11:00 ______

11:30 ______

12:00 ______

12:30 ______

MY EXTRAORDINARY NOTES

MY EXTRAORDINARY DAY PLANNER

M T W TH F SA SU --- JAN. FEB. MAR. APR. MAY JUN. JUL. AUG. SEPT. OCT. NOV. DEC.

1 2 3 4 5 6 7 8 9 10 11 12 13 14 15 16 17 18 19 20 21 22 23 24 25 26 27 28 29 30 31

MY TOP 4 EXTRAORDINARY PRIORITIES

- [ ]
- [ ]
- [ ]
- [ ]

MY EXTRAORDINARY PROJECTS

- [ ]
- [ ]
- [ ]
- [ ]

EXTRAORDINARY PEOPLE

- [ ]
- [ ]
- [ ]
- [ ]
- [ ]
- [ ]
- [ ]
- [ ]
- [ ]
- [ ]

MY EXTRAORDINARY TASKS

- [ ]
- [ ]
- [ ]
- [ ]

MY EXTRAORDINARY HABITS

- [ ]
- [ ]
- [ ]
- [ ]

MY EXTRAORDINARY APPOINTMENTS

5:00 __________
5:30 __________
6:00 __________
6:30 __________
7:00 __________
7:30 __________
8:00 __________
8:30 __________
9:00 __________
9:30 __________
10:00 __________
10:30 __________
11:00 __________
11:30 __________
12:00 __________
12:30 __________
1:00 __________
1:30 __________
2:00 __________
2:30 __________

3:00 __________
3:30 __________
4:00 __________
4:30 __________
5:00 __________
5:30 __________
6:00 __________
6:30 __________
7:00 __________
7:30 __________
8:00 __________
8:30 __________
9:00 __________
9:30 __________
10:00 __________
10:30 __________
11:00 __________
11:30 __________
12:00 __________
12:30 __________

MY EXTRAORDINARY NOTES

MY EXTRAORDINARY DAY PLANNER

M T W TH F SA SU --- JAN. FEB. MAR. APR. MAY JUN. JUL. AUG. SEPT. OCT. NOV. DEC.

1 2 3 4 5 6 7 8 9 10 11 12 13 14 15 16 17 18 19 20 21 22 23 24 25 26 27 28 29 30 31

MY TOP 4 EXTRAORDINARY PRIORITIES

- [ ]
- [ ]
- [ ]
- [ ]

MY EXTRAORDINARY PROJECTS

- [ ]
- [ ]
- [ ]
- [ ]

EXTRAORDINARY PEOPLE

- [ ]
- [ ]
- [ ]
- [ ]
- [ ]
- [ ]
- [ ]
- [ ]
- [ ]
- [ ]

MY EXTRAORDINARY TASKS

- [ ]
- [ ]
- [ ]
- [ ]

MY EXTRAORDINARY HABITS

- [ ]
- [ ]
- [ ]
- [ ]

MY EXTRAORDINARY APPOINTMENTS

5:00 ____
5:30 ____
6:00 ____
6:30 ____
7:00 ____
7:30 ____
8:00 ____
8:30 ____
9:00 ____
9:30 ____
10:00 ____
10:30 ____
11:00 ____
11:30 ____
12:00 ____
12:30 ____
1:00 ____
1:30 ____
2:00 ____
2:30 ____
3:00 ____
3:30 ____
4:00 ____
4:30 ____
5:00 ____
5:30 ____
6:00 ____
6:30 ____
7:00 ____
7:30 ____
8:00 ____
8:30 ____
9:00 ____
9:30 ____
10:00 ____
10:30 ____
11:00 ____
11:30 ____
12:00 ____
12:30 ____

MY EXTRAORDINARY NOTES

MY EXTRAORDINARY DAY PLANNER

M T W TH F SA SU --- JAN. FEB. MAR. APR. MAY JUN. JUL. AUG. SEPT. OCT. NOV. DEC.

1 2 3 4 5 6 7 8 9 10 11 12 13 14 15 16 17 18 19 20 21 22 23 24 25 26 27 28 29 30 31

MY TOP 4 EXTRAORDINARY PRIORITIES

- [ ]
- [ ]
- [ ]
- [ ]

MY EXTRAORDINARY PROJECTS

- [ ]
- [ ]
- [ ]
- [ ]

EXTRAORDINARY PEOPLE

- [ ]
- [ ]
- [ ]
- [ ]
- [ ]
- [ ]
- [ ]
- [ ]
- [ ]
- [ ]

MY EXTRAORDINARY TASKS

- [ ]
- [ ]
- [ ]
- [ ]

MY EXTRAORDINARY HABITS

- [ ]
- [ ]
- [ ]
- [ ]

MY EXTRAORDINARY APPOINTMENTS

5:00 ____

5:30 ____

6:00 ____

6:30 ____

7:00 ____

7:30 ____

8:00 ____

8:30 ____

9:00 ____

9:30 ____

10:00 ____

10:30 ____

11:00 ____

11:30 ____

12:00 ____

12:30 ____

1:00 ____

1:30 ____

2:00 ____

2:30 ____

3:00 ____

3:30 ____

4:00 ____

4:30 ____

5:00 ____

5:30 ____

6:00 ____

6:30 ____

7:00 ____

7:30 ____

8:00 ____

8:30 ____

9:00 ____

9:30 ____

10:00 ____

10:30 ____

11:00 ____

11:30 ____

12:00 ____

12:30 ____

MY EXTRAORDINARY NOTES

MY EXTRAORDINARY DAY PLANNER

M T W TH F SA SU --- JAN. FEB. MAR. APR. MAY JUN. JUL. AUG. SEPT. OCT. NOV. DEC.

1 2 3 4 5 6 7 8 9 10 11 12 13 14 15 16 17 18 19 20 21 22 23 24 25 26 27 28 29 30 31

MY TOP 4 EXTRAORDINARY PRIORITIES

- [ ]
- [ ]
- [ ]
- [ ]

EXTRAORDINARY PEOPLE

- [ ]
- [ ]
- [ ]
- [ ]
- [ ]
- [ ]
- [ ]
- [ ]
- [ ]
- [ ]

MY EXTRAORDINARY TASKS

- [ ]
- [ ]
- [ ]
- [ ]

MY EXTRAORDINARY PROJECTS

- [ ]
- [ ]
- [ ]
- [ ]

MY EXTRAORDINARY HABITS

- [ ]
- [ ]
- [ ]
- [ ]

MY EXTRAORDINARY APPOINTMENTS

5:00 ____
5:30 ____
6:00 ____
6:30 ____
7:00 ____
7:30 ____
8:00 ____
8:30 ____
9:00 ____
9:30 ____
10:00 ____
10:30 ____
11:00 ____
11:30 ____
12:00 ____
12:30 ____
1:00 ____
1:30 ____
2:00 ____
2:30 ____
3:00 ____
3:30 ____
4:00 ____
4:30 ____
5:00 ____
5:30 ____
6:00 ____
6:30 ____
7:00 ____
7:30 ____
8:00 ____
8:30 ____
9:00 ____
9:30 ____
10:00 ____
10:30 ____
11:00 ____
11:30 ____
12:00 ____
12:30 ____

MY EXTRAORDINARY NOTES

MY EXTRAORDINARY DAY PLANNER

M T W TH F SA SU --- JAN. FEB. MAR. APR. MAY JUN. JUL. AUG. SEPT. OCT. NOV. DEC.

1 2 3 4 5 6 7 8 9 10 11 12 13 14 15 16 17 18 19 20 21 22 23 24 25 26 27 28 29 30 31

MY TOP 4 EXTRAORDINARY PRIORITIES

- [ ]
- [ ]
- [ ]
- [ ]

EXTRAORDINARY PEOPLE

- [ ]
- [ ]
- [ ]
- [ ]
- [ ]
- [ ]
- [ ]
- [ ]
- [ ]
- [ ]

MY EXTRAORDINARY TASKS

- [ ]
- [ ]
- [ ]
- [ ]

MY EXTRAORDINARY PROJECTS

- [ ]
- [ ]
- [ ]
- [ ]

MY EXTRAORDINARY HABITS

- [ ]
- [ ]
- [ ]
- [ ]

MY EXTRAORDINARY APPOINTMENTS

5:00 ____
5:30 ____
6:00 ____
6:30 ____
7:00 ____
7:30 ____
8:00 ____
8:30 ____
9:00 ____
9:30 ____
10:00 ____
10:30 ____
11:00 ____
11:30 ____
12:00 ____
12:30 ____
1:00 ____
1:30 ____
2:00 ____
2:30 ____
3:00 ____
3:30 ____
4:00 ____
4:30 ____
5:00 ____
5:30 ____
6:00 ____
6:30 ____
7:00 ____
7:30 ____
8:00 ____
8:30 ____
9:00 ____
9:30 ____
10:00 ____
10:30 ____
11:00 ____
11:30 ____
12:00 ____
12:30 ____

MY EXTRAORDINARY NOTES

MY EXTRAORDINARY 30-DAY REVIEW

Week of: ______________________________

Month of: ______________________________

The "WINS" for this past week/month were:

____

____

____

What I did not get done, but intended to do:

____

____

____

Challenges, situations, and/or problems I am facing now:

____

____

____

MY EXTRAORDINARY 30-DAY REVIEW

Opportunities I see for myself right now:

What I will do before the end of this coming week/month:

Notes:

MY EXTRAORDINARY DAY PLANNER

M T W TH F SA SU --- JAN. FEB. MAR. APR. MAY JUN. JUL. AUG. SEPT. OCT. NOV. DEC.

1 2 3 4 5 6 7 8 9 10 11 12 13 14 15 16 17 18 19 20 21 22 23 24 25 26 27 28 29 30 31

MY TOP 4 EXTRAORDINARY PRIORITIES

- ☐
- ☐
- ☐
- ☐

MY EXTRAORDINARY PROJECTS

- ☐
- ☐
- ☐
- ☐

EXTRAORDINARY PEOPLE

- ☐
- ☐
- ☐
- ☐
- ☐
- ☐
- ☐
- ☐
- ☐
- ☐

MY EXTRAORDINARY TASKS

- ☐
- ☐
- ☐
- ☐

MY EXTRAORDINARY HABITS

- ☐
- ☐
- ☐
- ☐

MY EXTRAORDINARY APPOINTMENTS

5:00 ____________________
5:30 ____________________
6:00 ____________________
6:30 ____________________
7:00 ____________________
7:30 ____________________
8:00 ____________________
8:30 ____________________
9:00 ____________________
9:30 ____________________
10:00 ____________________
10:30 ____________________
11:00 ____________________
11:30 ____________________
12:00 ____________________
12:30 ____________________
1:00 ____________________
1:30 ____________________
2:00 ____________________
2:30 ____________________

3:00 ____________________
3:30 ____________________
4:00 ____________________
4:30 ____________________
5:00 ____________________
5:30 ____________________
6:00 ____________________
6:30 ____________________
7:00 ____________________
7:30 ____________________
8:00 ____________________
8:30 ____________________
9:00 ____________________
9:30 ____________________
10:00 ____________________
10:30 ____________________
11:00 ____________________
11:30 ____________________
12:00 ____________________
12:30 ____________________

MY EXTRAORDINARY NOTES

MY EXTRAORDINARY DAY PLANNER

M T W TH F SA SU --- JAN. FEB. MAR. APR. MAY JUN. JUL. AUG. SEPT. OCT. NOV. DEC.

1 2 3 4 5 6 7 8 9 10 11 12 13 14 15 16 17 18 19 20 21 22 23 24 25 26 27 28 29 30 31

MY TOP 4 EXTRAORDINARY PRIORITIES

- [ ]
- [ ]
- [ ]
- [ ]

MY EXTRAORDINARY PROJECTS

- [ ]
- [ ]
- [ ]
- [ ]

EXTRAORDINARY PEOPLE

- [ ]
- [ ]
- [ ]
- [ ]
- [ ]
- [ ]
- [ ]
- [ ]
- [ ]
- [ ]

MY EXTRAORDINARY TASKS

- [ ]
- [ ]
- [ ]
- [ ]

MY EXTRAORDINARY HABITS

- [ ]
- [ ]
- [ ]
- [ ]

MY EXTRAORDINARY APPOINTMENTS

5:00 __________
5:30
6:00
6:30
7:00
7:30
8:00
8:30
9:00
9:30
10:00
10:30
11:00
11:30
12:00
12:30
1:00
1:30
2:00
2:30

3:00
3:30
4:00
4:30
5:00
5:30
6:00
6:30
7:00
7:30
8:00
8:30
9:00
9:30
10:00
10:30
11:00
11:30
12:00
12:30

MY EXTRAORDINARY NOTES

MY EXTRAORDINARY DAY PLANNER

M T W TH F SA SU --- JAN. FEB. MAR. APR. MAY JUN. JUL. AUG. SEPT. OCT. NOV. DEC.

1 2 3 4 5 6 7 8 9 10 11 12 13 14 15 16 17 18 19 20 21 22 23 24 25 26 27 28 29 30 31

MY TOP 4 EXTRAORDINARY PRIORITIES

- ☐
- ☐
- ☐
- ☐

EXTRAORDINARY PEOPLE

- ☐
- ☐
- ☐
- ☐
- ☐
- ☐
- ☐
- ☐
- ☐
- ☐

MY EXTRAORDINARY TASKS

- ☐
- ☐
- ☐
- ☐

MY EXTRAORDINARY PROJECTS

- ☐
- ☐
- ☐
- ☐

MY EXTRAORDINARY HABITS

- ☐
- ☐
- ☐
- ☐

MY EXTRAORDINARY APPOINTMENTS

5:00 ______
5:30 ______
6:00 ______
6:30 ______
7:00 ______
7:30 ______
8:00 ______
8:30 ______
9:00 ______
9:30 ______
10:00 ______
10:30 ______
11:00 ______
11:30 ______
12:00 ______
12:30 ______
1:00 ______
1:30 ______
2:00 ______
2:30 ______

3:00 ______
3:30 ______
4:00 ______
4:30 ______
5:00 ______
5:30 ______
6:00 ______
6:30 ______
7:00 ______
7:30 ______
8:00 ______
8:30 ______
9:00 ______
9:30 ______
10:00 ______
10:30 ______
11:00 ______
11:30 ______
12:00 ______
12:30 ______

MY EXTRAORDINARY NOTES

MY EXTRAORDINARY DAY PLANNER

M T W TH F SA SU --- JAN. FEB. MAR. APR. MAY JUN. JUL. AUG. SEPT. OCT. NOV. DEC.

1 2 3 4 5 6 7 8 9 10 11 12 13 14 15 16 17 18 19 20 21 22 23 24 25 26 27 28 29 30 31

MY TOP 4 EXTRAORDINARY PRIORITIES

- ☐
- ☐
- ☐
- ☐

EXTRAORDINARY PEOPLE

- ☐
- ☐
- ☐
- ☐
- ☐
- ☐
- ☐
- ☐
- ☐
- ☐

MY EXTRAORDINARY TASKS

- ☐
- ☐
- ☐
- ☐

MY EXTRAORDINARY PROJECTS

- ☐
- ☐
- ☐
- ☐

MY EXTRAORDINARY HABITS

- ☐
- ☐
- ☐
- ☐

MY EXTRAORDINARY APPOINTMENTS

5:00		3:00	
5:30		3:30	
6:00		4:00	
6:30		4:30	
7:00		5:00	
7:30		5:30	
8:00		6:00	
8:30		6:30	
9:00		7:00	
9:30		7:30	
10:00		8:00	
10:30		8:30	
11:00		9:00	
11:30		9:30	
12:00		10:00	
12:30		10:30	
1:00		11:00	
1:30		11:30	
2:00		12:00	
2:30		12:30	

MY EXTRAORDINARY NOTES

MY EXTRAORDINARY DAY PLANNER

M T W TH F SA SU --- JAN. FEB. MAR. APR. MAY JUN. JUL. AUG. SEPT. OCT. NOV. DEC.

1 2 3 4 5 6 7 8 9 10 11 12 13 14 15 16 17 18 19 20 21 22 23 24 25 26 27 28 29 30 31

MY TOP 4 EXTRAORDINARY PRIORITIES

- [ ]
- [ ]
- [ ]
- [ ]

EXTRAORDINARY PEOPLE

- [ ]
- [ ]
- [ ]
- [ ]
- [ ]
- [ ]
- [ ]
- [ ]
- [ ]
- [ ]

MY EXTRAORDINARY TASKS

- [ ]
- [ ]
- [ ]
- [ ]

MY EXTRAORDINARY PROJECTS

- [ ]
- [ ]
- [ ]
- [ ]

MY EXTRAORDINARY HABITS

- [ ]
- [ ]
- [ ]
- [ ]

MY EXTRAORDINARY APPOINTMENTS

5:00		3:00	
5:30		3:30	
6:00		4:00	
6:30		4:30	
7:00		5:00	
7:30		5:30	
8:00		6:00	
8:30		6:30	
9:00		7:00	
9:30		7:30	
10:00		8:00	
10:30		8:30	
11:00		9:00	
11:30		9:30	
12:00		10:00	
12:30		10:30	
1:00		11:00	
1:30		11:30	
2:00		12:00	
2:30		12:30	

MY EXTRAORDINARY NOTES

MY EXTRAORDINARY DAY PLANNER

M T W TH F SA SU --- JAN. FEB. MAR. APR. MAY JUN. JUL. AUG. SEPT. OCT. NOV. DEC.

1 2 3 4 5 6 7 8 9 10 11 12 13 14 15 16 17 18 19 20 21 22 23 24 25 26 27 28 29 30 31

MY TOP 4 EXTRAORDINARY PRIORITIES

- [ ]
- [ ]
- [ ]
- [ ]

EXTRAORDINARY PEOPLE

- [ ]
- [ ]
- [ ]
- [ ]
- [ ]
- [ ]
- [ ]
- [ ]
- [ ]
- [ ]

MY EXTRAORDINARY TASKS

- [ ]
- [ ]
- [ ]
- [ ]

MY EXTRAORDINARY PROJECTS

- [ ]
- [ ]
- [ ]
- [ ]

MY EXTRAORDINARY HABITS

- [ ]
- [ ]
- [ ]
- [ ]

MY EXTRAORDINARY APPOINTMENTS

5:00 __________
5:30 __________
6:00 __________
6:30 __________
7:00 __________
7:30 __________
8:00 __________
8:30 __________
9:00 __________
9:30 __________
10:00 __________
10:30 __________
11:00 __________
11:30 __________
12:00 __________
12:30 __________
1:00 __________
1:30 __________
2:00 __________
2:30 __________
3:00 __________
3:30 __________
4:00 __________
4:30 __________
5:00 __________
5:30 __________
6:00 __________
6:30 __________
7:00 __________
7:30 __________
8:00 __________
8:30 __________
9:00 __________
9:30 __________
10:00 __________
10:30 __________
11:00 __________
11:30 __________
12:00 __________
12:30 __________

MY EXTRAORDINARY NOTES

MY EXTRAORDINARY DAY PLANNER

M T W TH F SA SU --- JAN. FEB. MAR. APR. MAY JUN. JUL. AUG. SEPT. OCT. NOV. DEC.

1 2 3 4 5 6 7 8 9 10 11 12 13 14 15 16 17 18 19 20 21 22 23 24 25 26 27 28 29 30 31

MY TOP 4 EXTRAORDINARY PRIORITIES

- [ ]
- [ ]
- [ ]
- [ ]

EXTRAORDINARY PEOPLE

- [ ]
- [ ]
- [ ]
- [ ]
- [ ]
- [ ]
- [ ]
- [ ]
- [ ]
- [ ]

MY EXTRAORDINARY TASKS

- [ ]
- [ ]
- [ ]
- [ ]

MY EXTRAORDINARY PROJECTS

- [ ]
- [ ]
- [ ]
- [ ]

MY EXTRAORDINARY HABITS

- [ ]
- [ ]
- [ ]
- [ ]

MY EXTRAORDINARY APPOINTMENTS

Time		Time	
5:00		3:00	
5:30		3:30	
6:00		4:00	
6:30		4:30	
7:00		5:00	
7:30		5:30	
8:00		6:00	
8:30		6:30	
9:00		7:00	
9:30		7:30	
10:00		8:00	
10:30		8:30	
11:00		9:00	
11:30		9:30	
12:00		10:00	
12:30		10:30	
1:00		11:00	
1:30		11:30	
2:00		12:00	
2:30		12:30	

MY EXTRAORDINARY NOTES

MY EXTRAORDINARY DAY PLANNER

M T W TH F SA SU --- JAN. FEB. MAR. APR. MAY JUN. JUL. AUG. SEPT. OCT. NOV. DEC.

1 2 3 4 5 6 7 8 9 10 11 12 13 14 15 16 17 18 19 20 21 22 23 24 25 26 27 28 29 30 31

MY TOP 4 EXTRAORDINARY PRIORITIES

- ☐
- ☐
- ☐
- ☐

EXTRAORDINARY PEOPLE

- ☐
- ☐
- ☐
- ☐
- ☐
- ☐
- ☐
- ☐
- ☐
- ☐

MY EXTRAORDINARY TASKS

- ☐
- ☐
- ☐
- ☐

MY EXTRAORDINARY PROJECTS

- ☐
- ☐
- ☐
- ☐

MY EXTRAORDINARY HABITS

- ☐
- ☐
- ☐
- ☐

MY EXTRAORDINARY APPOINTMENTS

5:00		3:00	
5:30		3:30	
6:00		4:00	
6:30		4:30	
7:00		5:00	
7:30		5:30	
8:00		6:00	
8:30		6:30	
9:00		7:00	
9:30		7:30	
10:00		8:00	
10:30		8:30	
11:00		9:00	
11:30		9:30	
12:00		10:00	
12:30		10:30	
1:00		11:00	
1:30		11:30	
2:00		12:00	
2:30		12:30	

MY EXTRAORDINARY NOTES

MY EXTRAORDINARY DAY PLANNER

M T W TH F SA SU --- JAN. FEB. MAR. APR. MAY JUN. JUL. AUG. SEPT. OCT. NOV. DEC.

1 2 3 4 5 6 7 8 9 10 11 12 13 14 15 16 17 18 19 20 21 22 23 24 25 26 27 28 29 30 31

MY TOP 4 EXTRAORDINARY PRIORITIES

- [ ]
- [ ]
- [ ]
- [ ]

EXTRAORDINARY PEOPLE

- [ ]
- [ ]
- [ ]
- [ ]
- [ ]
- [ ]
- [ ]
- [ ]
- [ ]
- [ ]

MY EXTRAORDINARY TASKS

- [ ]
- [ ]
- [ ]
- [ ]

MY EXTRAORDINARY PROJECTS

- [ ]
- [ ]
- [ ]
- [ ]

MY EXTRAORDINARY HABITS

- [ ]
- [ ]
- [ ]
- [ ]

MY EXTRAORDINARY APPOINTMENTS

5:00		3:00	
5:30		3:30	
6:00		4:00	
6:30		4:30	
7:00		5:00	
7:30		5:30	
8:00		6:00	
8:30		6:30	
9:00		7:00	
9:30		7:30	
10:00		8:00	
10:30		8:30	
11:00		9:00	
11:30		9:30	
12:00		10:00	
12:30		10:30	
1:00		11:00	
1:30		11:30	
2:00		12:00	
2:30		12:30	

MY EXTRAORDINARY NOTES

MY EXTRAORDINARY DAY PLANNER

M T W TH F SA SU --- JAN. FEB. MAR. APR. MAY JUN. JUL. AUG. SEPT. OCT. NOV. DEC.

1 2 3 4 5 6 7 8 9 10 11 12 13 14 15 16 17 18 19 20 21 22 23 24 25 26 27 28 29 30 31

MY TOP 4 EXTRAORDINARY PRIORITIES

- [ ]
- [ ]
- [ ]
- [ ]

EXTRAORDINARY PEOPLE

- [ ]
- [ ]
- [ ]
- [ ]
- [ ]
- [ ]
- [ ]
- [ ]
- [ ]
- [ ]

MY EXTRAORDINARY TASKS

- [ ]
- [ ]
- [ ]
- [ ]

MY EXTRAORDINARY PROJECTS

- [ ]
- [ ]
- [ ]
- [ ]

MY EXTRAORDINARY HABITS

- [ ]
- [ ]
- [ ]
- [ ]

MY EXTRAORDINARY APPOINTMENTS

5:00		3:00	
5:30		3:30	
6:00		4:00	
6:30		4:30	
7:00		5:00	
7:30		5:30	
8:00		6:00	
8:30		6:30	
9:00		7:00	
9:30		7:30	
10:00		8:00	
10:30		8:30	
11:00		9:00	
11:30		9:30	
12:00		10:00	
12:30		10:30	
1:00		11:00	
1:30		11:30	
2:00		12:00	
2:30		12:30	

MY EXTRAORDINARY NOTES

MY EXTRAORDINARY DAY PLANNER

M T W TH F SA SU --- JAN. FEB. MAR. APR. MAY JUN. JUL. AUG. SEPT. OCT. NOV. DEC.

1 2 3 4 5 6 7 8 9 10 11 12 13 14 15 16 17 18 19 20 21 22 23 24 25 26 27 28 29 30 31

MY TOP 4 EXTRAORDINARY PRIORITIES

- [ ]
- [ ]
- [ ]
- [ ]

EXTRAORDINARY PEOPLE

- [ ]
- [ ]
- [ ]
- [ ]
- [ ]
- [ ]
- [ ]
- [ ]
- [ ]
- [ ]

MY EXTRAORDINARY TASKS

- [ ]
- [ ]
- [ ]
- [ ]

MY EXTRAORDINARY PROJECTS

- [ ]
- [ ]
- [ ]
- [ ]

MY EXTRAORDINARY HABITS

- [ ]
- [ ]
- [ ]
- [ ]

MY EXTRAORDINARY APPOINTMENTS

5:00		3:00	
5:30		3:30	
6:00		4:00	
6:30		4:30	
7:00		5:00	
7:30		5:30	
8:00		6:00	
8:30		6:30	
9:00		7:00	
9:30		7:30	
10:00		8:00	
10:30		8:30	
11:00		9:00	
11:30		9:30	
12:00		10:00	
12:30		10:30	
1:00		11:00	
1:30		11:30	
2:00		12:00	
2:30		12:30	

MY EXTRAORDINARY NOTES

MY EXTRAORDINARY DAY PLANNER

M T W TH F SA SU --- JAN. FEB. MAR. APR. MAY JUN. JUL. AUG. SEPT. OCT. NOV. DEC.

1 2 3 4 5 6 7 8 9 10 11 12 13 14 15 16 17 18 19 20 21 22 23 24 25 26 27 28 29 30 31

MY TOP 4 EXTRAORDINARY PRIORITIES

- [ ]
- [ ]
- [ ]
- [ ]

EXTRAORDINARY PEOPLE

- [ ]
- [ ]
- [ ]
- [ ]
- [ ]
- [ ]
- [ ]
- [ ]
- [ ]
- [ ]

MY EXTRAORDINARY TASKS

- [ ]
- [ ]
- [ ]
- [ ]

MY EXTRAORDINARY PROJECTS

- [ ]
- [ ]
- [ ]
- [ ]

MY EXTRAORDINARY HABITS

- [ ]
- [ ]
- [ ]
- [ ]

MY EXTRAORDINARY APPOINTMENTS

5:00		3:00	
5:30		3:30	
6:00		4:00	
6:30		4:30	
7:00		5:00	
7:30		5:30	
8:00		6:00	
8:30		6:30	
9:00		7:00	
9:30		7:30	
10:00		8:00	
10:30		8:30	
11:00		9:00	
11:30		9:30	
12:00		10:00	
12:30		10:30	
1:00		11:00	
1:30		11:30	
2:00		12:00	
2:30		12:30	

MY EXTRAORDINARY NOTES

MY EXTRAORDINARY DAY PLANNER

M T W TH F SA SU --- JAN. FEB. MAR. APR. MAY JUN. JUL. AUG. SEPT. OCT. NOV. DEC.

1 2 3 4 5 6 7 8 9 10 11 12 13 14 15 16 17 18 19 20 21 22 23 24 25 26 27 28 29 30 31

MY TOP 4 EXTRAORDINARY PRIORITIES

- [ ]
- [ ]
- [ ]
- [ ]

EXTRAORDINARY PEOPLE

- [ ]
- [ ]
- [ ]
- [ ]
- [ ]
- [ ]
- [ ]
- [ ]
- [ ]
- [ ]

MY EXTRAORDINARY TASKS

- [ ]
- [ ]
- [ ]
- [ ]

MY EXTRAORDINARY PROJECTS

- [ ]
- [ ]
- [ ]
- [ ]

MY EXTRAORDINARY HABITS

- [ ]
- [ ]
- [ ]
- [ ]

MY EXTRAORDINARY APPOINTMENTS

5:00 ______
5:30 ______
6:00 ______
6:30 ______
7:00 ______
7:30 ______
8:00 ______
8:30 ______
9:00 ______
9:30 ______
10:00 ______
10:30 ______
11:00 ______
11:30 ______
12:00 ______
12:30 ______
1:00 ______
1:30 ______
2:00 ______
2:30 ______
3:00 ______
3:30 ______
4:00 ______
4:30 ______
5:00 ______
5:30 ______
6:00 ______
6:30 ______
7:00 ______
7:30 ______
8:00 ______
8:30 ______
9:00 ______
9:30 ______
10:00 ______
10:30 ______
11:00 ______
11:30 ______
12:00 ______
12:30 ______

MY EXTRAORDINARY NOTES

MY EXTRAORDINARY DAY PLANNER

M T W TH F SA SU --- JAN. FEB. MAR. APR. MAY JUN. JUL. AUG. SEPT. OCT. NOV. DEC.

1 2 3 4 5 6 7 8 9 10 11 12 13 14 15 16 17 18 19 20 21 22 23 24 25 26 27 28 29 30 31

MY TOP 4 EXTRAORDINARY PRIORITIES

- [ ]
- [ ]
- [ ]
- [ ]

EXTRAORDINARY PEOPLE

- [ ]
- [ ]
- [ ]
- [ ]
- [ ]
- [ ]
- [ ]
- [ ]
- [ ]
- [ ]

MY EXTRAORDINARY TASKS

- [ ]
- [ ]
- [ ]
- [ ]

MY EXTRAORDINARY PROJECTS

- [ ]
- [ ]
- [ ]
- [ ]

MY EXTRAORDINARY HABITS

- [ ]
- [ ]
- [ ]
- [ ]

MY EXTRAORDINARY APPOINTMENTS

5:00		3:00	
5:30		3:30	
6:00		4:00	
6:30		4:30	
7:00		5:00	
7:30		5:30	
8:00		6:00	
8:30		6:30	
9:00		7:00	
9:30		7:30	
10:00		8:00	
10:30		8:30	
11:00		9:00	
11:30		9:30	
12:00		10:00	
12:30		10:30	
1:00		11:00	
1:30		11:30	
2:00		12:00	
2:30		12:30	

MY EXTRAORDINARY NOTES

MY EXTRAORDINARY DAY PLANNER

M T W TH F SA SU --- JAN. FEB. MAR. APR. MAY JUN. JUL. AUG. SEPT. OCT. NOV. DEC.

1 2 3 4 5 6 7 8 9 10 11 12 13 14 15 16 17 18 19 20 21 22 23 24 25 26 27 28 29 30 31

MY TOP 4 EXTRAORDINARY PRIORITIES

- [ ]
- [ ]
- [ ]
- [ ]

EXTRAORDINARY PEOPLE

- [ ]
- [ ]
- [ ]
- [ ]
- [ ]
- [ ]
- [ ]
- [ ]
- [ ]
- [ ]

MY EXTRAORDINARY TASKS

- [ ]
- [ ]
- [ ]
- [ ]

MY EXTRAORDINARY PROJECTS

- [ ]
- [ ]
- [ ]
- [ ]

MY EXTRAORDINARY HABITS

- [ ]
- [ ]
- [ ]
- [ ]

MY EXTRAORDINARY APPOINTMENTS

5:00		3:00	
5:30		3:30	
6:00		4:00	
6:30		4:30	
7:00		5:00	
7:30		5:30	
8:00		6:00	
8:30		6:30	
9:00		7:00	
9:30		7:30	
10:00		8:00	
10:30		8:30	
11:00		9:00	
11:30		9:30	
12:00		10:00	
12:30		10:30	
1:00		11:00	
1:30		11:30	
2:00		12:00	
2:30		12:30	

MY EXTRAORDINARY NOTES

MY EXTRAORDINARY DAY PLANNER

M T W TH F SA SU --- JAN. FEB. MAR. APR. MAY JUN. JUL. AUG. SEPT. OCT. NOV. DEC.

1 2 3 4 5 6 7 8 9 10 11 12 13 14 15 16 17 18 19 20 21 22 23 24 25 26 27 28 29 30 31

MY TOP 4 EXTRAORDINARY PRIORITIES

- ☐
- ☐
- ☐
- ☐

EXTRAORDINARY PEOPLE

- ☐
- ☐
- ☐
- ☐
- ☐
- ☐
- ☐
- ☐
- ☐
- ☐

MY EXTRAORDINARY TASKS

- ☐
- ☐
- ☐
- ☐

MY EXTRAORDINARY PROJECTS

- ☐
- ☐
- ☐
- ☐

MY EXTRAORDINARY HABITS

- ☐
- ☐
- ☐
- ☐

MY EXTRAORDINARY APPOINTMENTS

5:00		3:00	
5:30		3:30	
6:00		4:00	
6:30		4:30	
7:00		5:00	
7:30		5:30	
8:00		6:00	
8:30		6:30	
9:00		7:00	
9:30		7:30	
10:00		8:00	
10:30		8:30	
11:00		9:00	
11:30		9:30	
12:00		10:00	
12:30		10:30	
1:00		11:00	
1:30		11:30	
2:00		12:00	
2:30		12:30	

MY EXTRAORDINARY NOTES

MY EXTRAORDINARY DAY PLANNER

M T W TH F SA SU --- JAN. FEB. MAR. APR. MAY JUN. JUL. AUG. SEPT. OCT. NOV. DEC.

1 2 3 4 5 6 7 8 9 10 11 12 13 14 15 16 17 18 19 20 21 22 23 24 25 26 27 28 29 30 31

MY TOP 4 EXTRAORDINARY PRIORITIES	EXTRAORDINARY PEOPLE	MY EXTRAORDINARY TASKS
☐ ☐ ☐ ☐	☐ ☐ ☐ ☐ ☐ ☐ ☐ ☐ ☐ ☐	☐ ☐ ☐ ☐
MY EXTRAORDINARY PROJECTS		MY EXTRAORDINARY HABITS
☐ ☐ ☐ ☐		☐ ☐ ☐ ☐

MY EXTRAORDINARY APPOINTMENTS

5:00		3:00	
5:30		3:30	
6:00		4:00	
6:30		4:30	
7:00		5:00	
7:30		5:30	
8:00		6:00	
8:30		6:30	
9:00		7:00	
9:30		7:30	
10:00		8:00	
10:30		8:30	
11:00		9:00	
11:30		9:30	
12:00		10:00	
12:30		10:30	
1:00		11:00	
1:30		11:30	
2:00		12:00	
2:30		12:30	

MY EXTRAORDINARY NOTES

MY EXTRAORDINARY DAY PLANNER

M T W TH F SA SU --- JAN. FEB. MAR. APR. MAY JUN. JUL. AUG. SEPT. OCT. NOV. DEC.

1 2 3 4 5 6 7 8 9 10 11 12 13 14 15 16 17 18 19 20 21 22 23 24 25 26 27 28 29 30 31

MY TOP 4 EXTRAORDINARY PRIORITIES

- [ ]
- [ ]
- [ ]
- [ ]

EXTRAORDINARY PEOPLE

- [ ]
- [ ]
- [ ]
- [ ]
- [ ]
- [ ]
- [ ]
- [ ]
- [ ]
- [ ]

MY EXTRAORDINARY TASKS

- [ ]
- [ ]
- [ ]
- [ ]

MY EXTRAORDINARY PROJECTS

- [ ]
- [ ]
- [ ]
- [ ]

MY EXTRAORDINARY HABITS

- [ ]
- [ ]
- [ ]
- [ ]

MY EXTRAORDINARY APPOINTMENTS

5:00 ______
5:30 ______
6:00 ______
6:30 ______
7:00 ______
7:30 ______
8:00 ______
8:30 ______
9:00 ______
9:30 ______
10:00 ______
10:30 ______
11:00 ______
11:30 ______
12:00 ______
12:30 ______
1:00 ______
1:30 ______
2:00 ______
2:30 ______
3:00 ______
3:30 ______
4:00 ______
4:30 ______
5:00 ______
5:30 ______
6:00 ______
6:30 ______
7:00 ______
7:30 ______
8:00 ______
8:30 ______
9:00 ______
9:30 ______
10:00 ______
10:30 ______
11:00 ______
11:30 ______
12:00 ______
12:30 ______

MY EXTRAORDINARY NOTES

MY EXTRAORDINARY DAY PLANNER

M T W TH F SA SU --- JAN. FEB. MAR. APR. MAY JUN. JUL. AUG. SEPT. OCT. NOV. DEC.

1 2 3 4 5 6 7 8 9 10 11 12 13 14 15 16 17 18 19 20 21 22 23 24 25 26 27 28 29 30 31

MY TOP 4 EXTRAORDINARY PRIORITIES

- [ ]
- [ ]
- [ ]
- [ ]

EXTRAORDINARY PEOPLE

- [ ]
- [ ]
- [ ]
- [ ]
- [ ]
- [ ]
- [ ]
- [ ]
- [ ]
- [ ]

MY EXTRAORDINARY TASKS

- [ ]
- [ ]
- [ ]
- [ ]

MY EXTRAORDINARY PROJECTS

- [ ]
- [ ]
- [ ]
- [ ]

MY EXTRAORDINARY HABITS

- [ ]
- [ ]
- [ ]
- [ ]

MY EXTRAORDINARY APPOINTMENTS

5:00 ______
5:30 ______
6:00 ______
6:30 ______
7:00 ______
7:30 ______
8:00 ______
8:30 ______
9:00 ______
9:30 ______
10:00 ______
10:30 ______
11:00 ______
11:30 ______
12:00 ______
12:30 ______
1:00 ______
1:30 ______
2:00 ______
2:30 ______

3:00 ______
3:30 ______
4:00 ______
4:30 ______
5:00 ______
5:30 ______
6:00 ______
6:30 ______
7:00 ______
7:30 ______
8:00 ______
8:30 ______
9:00 ______
9:30 ______
10:00 ______
10:30 ______
11:00 ______
11:30 ______
12:00 ______
12:30 ______

MY EXTRAORDINARY NOTES

MY EXTRAORDINARY DAY PLANNER

M T W TH F SA SU --- JAN. FEB. MAR. APR. MAY JUN. JUL. AUG. SEPT. OCT. NOV. DEC.

1 2 3 4 5 6 7 8 9 10 11 12 13 14 15 16 17 18 19 20 21 22 23 24 25 26 27 28 29 30 31

MY TOP 4 EXTRAORDINARY PRIORITIES

- ☐
- ☐
- ☐
- ☐

EXTRAORDINARY PEOPLE

- ☐
- ☐
- ☐
- ☐
- ☐
- ☐
- ☐
- ☐
- ☐
- ☐

MY EXTRAORDINARY TASKS

- ☐
- ☐
- ☐
- ☐

MY EXTRAORDINARY PROJECTS

- ☐
- ☐
- ☐
- ☐

MY EXTRAORDINARY HABITS

- ☐
- ☐
- ☐
- ☐

MY EXTRAORDINARY APPOINTMENTS

5:00		3:00	
5:30		3:30	
6:00		4:00	
6:30		4:30	
7:00		5:00	
7:30		5:30	
8:00		6:00	
8:30		6:30	
9:00		7:00	
9:30		7:30	
10:00		8:00	
10:30		8:30	
11:00		9:00	
11:30		9:30	
12:00		10:00	
12:30		10:30	
1:00		11:00	
1:30		11:30	
2:00		12:00	
2:30		12:30	

MY EXTRAORDINARY NOTES

MY EXTRAORDINARY DAY PLANNER

M T W TH F SA SU --- JAN. FEB. MAR. APR. MAY JUN. JUL. AUG. SEPT. OCT. NOV. DEC.

1 2 3 4 5 6 7 8 9 10 11 12 13 14 15 16 17 18 19 20 21 22 23 24 25 26 27 28 29 30 31

MY TOP 4 EXTRAORDINARY PRIORITIES

- [ ]
- [ ]
- [ ]
- [ ]

EXTRAORDINARY PEOPLE

- [ ]
- [ ]
- [ ]
- [ ]
- [ ]
- [ ]
- [ ]
- [ ]
- [ ]
- [ ]

MY EXTRAORDINARY TASKS

- [ ]
- [ ]
- [ ]
- [ ]

MY EXTRAORDINARY PROJECTS

- [ ]
- [ ]
- [ ]
- [ ]

MY EXTRAORDINARY HABITS

- [ ]
- [ ]
- [ ]
- [ ]

MY EXTRAORDINARY APPOINTMENTS

5:00 ____
5:30 ____
6:00 ____
6:30 ____
7:00 ____
7:30 ____
8:00 ____
8:30 ____
9:00 ____
9:30 ____
10:00 ____
10:30 ____
11:00 ____
11:30 ____
12:00 ____
12:30 ____
1:00 ____
1:30 ____
2:00 ____
2:30 ____

3:00 ____
3:30 ____
4:00 ____
4:30 ____
5:00 ____
5:30 ____
6:00 ____
6:30 ____
7:00 ____
7:30 ____
8:00 ____
8:30 ____
9:00 ____
9:30 ____
10:00 ____
10:30 ____
11:00 ____
11:30 ____
12:00 ____
12:30 ____

MY EXTRAORDINARY NOTES

MY EXTRAORDINARY DAY PLANNER

M T W TH F SA SU --- JAN. FEB. MAR. APR. MAY JUN. JUL. AUG. SEPT. OCT. NOV. DEC.

1 2 3 4 5 6 7 8 9 10 11 12 13 14 15 16 17 18 19 20 21 22 23 24 25 26 27 28 29 30 31

MY TOP 4 EXTRAORDINARY PRIORITIES

- [ ]
- [ ]
- [ ]
- [ ]

EXTRAORDINARY PEOPLE

- [ ]
- [ ]
- [ ]
- [ ]
- [ ]
- [ ]
- [ ]
- [ ]
- [ ]
- [ ]

MY EXTRAORDINARY TASKS

- [ ]
- [ ]
- [ ]
- [ ]

MY EXTRAORDINARY PROJECTS

- [ ]
- [ ]
- [ ]
- [ ]

MY EXTRAORDINARY HABITS

- [ ]
- [ ]
- [ ]
- [ ]

MY EXTRAORDINARY APPOINTMENTS

5:00	3:00
5:30	3:30
6:00	4:00
6:30	4:30
7:00	5:00
7:30	5:30
8:00	6:00
8:30	6:30
9:00	7:00
9:30	7:30
10:00	8:00
10:30	8:30
11:00	9:00
11:30	9:30
12:00	10:00
12:30	10:30
1:00	11:00
1:30	11:30
2:00	12:00
2:30	12:30

MY EXTRAORDINARY NOTES

MY EXTRAORDINARY DAY PLANNER

M T W TH F SA SU --- JAN. FEB. MAR. APR. MAY JUN. JUL. AUG. SEPT. OCT. NOV. DEC.

1 2 3 4 5 6 7 8 9 10 11 12 13 14 15 16 17 18 19 20 21 22 23 24 25 26 27 28 29 30 31

MY TOP 4 EXTRAORDINARY PRIORITIES

- [ ]
- [ ]
- [ ]
- [ ]

EXTRAORDINARY PEOPLE

- [ ]
- [ ]
- [ ]
- [ ]
- [ ]
- [ ]
- [ ]
- [ ]
- [ ]
- [ ]

MY EXTRAORDINARY TASKS

- [ ]
- [ ]
- [ ]
- [ ]

MY EXTRAORDINARY PROJECTS

- [ ]
- [ ]
- [ ]
- [ ]

MY EXTRAORDINARY HABITS

- [ ]
- [ ]
- [ ]
- [ ]

MY EXTRAORDINARY APPOINTMENTS

5:00 ______
5:30 ______
6:00 ______
6:30 ______
7:00 ______
7:30 ______
8:00 ______
8:30 ______
9:00 ______
9:30 ______
10:00 ______
10:30 ______
11:00 ______
11:30 ______
12:00 ______
12:30 ______
1:00 ______
1:30 ______
2:00 ______
2:30 ______
3:00 ______
3:30 ______
4:00 ______
4:30 ______
5:00 ______
5:30 ______
6:00 ______
6:30 ______
7:00 ______
7:30 ______
8:00 ______
8:30 ______
9:00 ______
9:30 ______
10:00 ______
10:30 ______
11:00 ______
11:30 ______
12:00 ______
12:30 ______

MY EXTRAORDINARY NOTES

MY EXTRAORDINARY DAY PLANNER

M T W TH F SA SU --- JAN. FEB. MAR. APR. MAY JUN. JUL. AUG. SEPT. OCT. NOV. DEC.

1 2 3 4 5 6 7 8 9 10 11 12 13 14 15 16 17 18 19 20 21 22 23 24 25 26 27 28 29 30 31

MY TOP 4 EXTRAORDINARY PRIORITIES

- [ ]
- [ ]
- [ ]
- [ ]

EXTRAORDINARY PEOPLE

- [ ]
- [ ]
- [ ]
- [ ]
- [ ]
- [ ]
- [ ]
- [ ]
- [ ]
- [ ]

MY EXTRAORDINARY TASKS

- [ ]
- [ ]
- [ ]
- [ ]

MY EXTRAORDINARY PROJECTS

- [ ]
- [ ]
- [ ]
- [ ]

MY EXTRAORDINARY HABITS

- [ ]
- [ ]
- [ ]
- [ ]

MY EXTRAORDINARY APPOINTMENTS

5:00 ______
5:30 ______
6:00 ______
6:30 ______
7:00 ______
7:30 ______
8:00 ______
8:30 ______
9:00 ______
9:30 ______
10:00 ______
10:30 ______
11:00 ______
11:30 ______
12:00 ______
12:30 ______
1:00 ______
1:30 ______
2:00 ______
2:30 ______
3:00 ______
3:30 ______
4:00 ______
4:30 ______
5:00 ______
5:30 ______
6:00 ______
6:30 ______
7:00 ______
7:30 ______
8:00 ______
8:30 ______
9:00 ______
9:30 ______
10:00 ______
10:30 ______
11:00 ______
11:30 ______
12:00 ______
12:30 ______

MY EXTRAORDINARY NOTES

MY EXTRAORDINARY DAY PLANNER

M T W TH F SA SU --- JAN. FEB. MAR. APR. MAY JUN. JUL. AUG. SEPT. OCT. NOV. DEC.

1 2 3 4 5 6 7 8 9 10 11 12 13 14 15 16 17 18 19 20 21 22 23 24 25 26 27 28 29 30 31

MY TOP 4 EXTRAORDINARY PRIORITIES

- ☐
- ☐
- ☐
- ☐

MY EXTRAORDINARY PROJECTS

- ☐
- ☐
- ☐
- ☐

EXTRAORDINARY PEOPLE

- ☐
- ☐
- ☐
- ☐
- ☐
- ☐
- ☐
- ☐
- ☐
- ☐

MY EXTRAORDINARY TASKS

- ☐
- ☐
- ☐
- ☐

MY EXTRAORDINARY HABITS

- ☐
- ☐
- ☐
- ☐

MY EXTRAORDINARY APPOINTMENTS

5:00 ______
5:30 ______
6:00 ______
6:30 ______
7:00 ______
7:30 ______
8:00 ______
8:30 ______
9:00 ______
9:30 ______
10:00 ______
10:30 ______
11:00 ______
11:30 ______
12:00 ______
12:30 ______
1:00 ______
1:30 ______
2:00 ______
2:30 ______
3:00 ______
3:30 ______
4:00 ______
4:30 ______
5:00 ______
5:30 ______
6:00 ______
6:30 ______
7:00 ______
7:30 ______
8:00 ______
8:30 ______
9:00 ______
9:30 ______
10:00 ______
10:30 ______
11:00 ______
11:30 ______
12:00 ______
12:30 ______

MY EXTRAORDINARY NOTES

MY EXTRAORDINARY DAY PLANNER

M T W TH F SA SU --- JAN. FEB. MAR. APR. MAY JUN. JUL. AUG. SEPT. OCT. NOV. DEC.

1 2 3 4 5 6 7 8 9 10 11 12 13 14 15 16 17 18 19 20 21 22 23 24 25 26 27 28 29 30 31

MY TOP 4 EXTRAORDINARY PRIORITIES

- [ ]
- [ ]
- [ ]
- [ ]

EXTRAORDINARY PEOPLE

- [ ]
- [ ]
- [ ]
- [ ]
- [ ]
- [ ]
- [ ]
- [ ]
- [ ]
- [ ]

MY EXTRAORDINARY TASKS

- [ ]
- [ ]
- [ ]
- [ ]

MY EXTRAORDINARY PROJECTS

- [ ]
- [ ]
- [ ]
- [ ]

MY EXTRAORDINARY HABITS

- [ ]
- [ ]
- [ ]
- [ ]

MY EXTRAORDINARY APPOINTMENTS

5:00		3:00	
5:30		3:30	
6:00		4:00	
6:30		4:30	
7:00		5:00	
7:30		5:30	
8:00		6:00	
8:30		6:30	
9:00		7:00	
9:30		7:30	
10:00		8:00	
10:30		8:30	
11:00		9:00	
11:30		9:30	
12:00		10:00	
12:30		10:30	
1:00		11:00	
1:30		11:30	
2:00		12:00	
2:30		12:30	

MY EXTRAORDINARY NOTES

MY EXTRAORDINARY DAY PLANNER

M T W TH F SA SU --- JAN. FEB. MAR. APR. MAY JUN. JUL. AUG. SEPT. OCT. NOV. DEC.

1 2 3 4 5 6 7 8 9 10 11 12 13 14 15 16 17 18 19 20 21 22 23 24 25 26 27 28 29 30 31

MY TOP 4 EXTRAORDINARY PRIORITIES

- [ ]
- [ ]
- [ ]
- [ ]

EXTRAORDINARY PEOPLE

- [ ]
- [ ]
- [ ]
- [ ]
- [ ]
- [ ]
- [ ]
- [ ]
- [ ]
- [ ]

MY EXTRAORDINARY TASKS

- [ ]
- [ ]
- [ ]
- [ ]

MY EXTRAORDINARY PROJECTS

- [ ]
- [ ]
- [ ]
- [ ]

MY EXTRAORDINARY HABITS

- [ ]
- [ ]
- [ ]
- [ ]

MY EXTRAORDINARY APPOINTMENTS

5:00		3:00	
5:30		3:30	
6:00		4:00	
6:30		4:30	
7:00		5:00	
7:30		5:30	
8:00		6:00	
8:30		6:30	
9:00		7:00	
9:30		7:30	
10:00		8:00	
10:30		8:30	
11:00		9:00	
11:30		9:30	
12:00		10:00	
12:30		10:30	
1:00		11:00	
1:30		11:30	
2:00		12:00	
2:30		12:30	

MY EXTRAORDINARY NOTES

MY EXTRAORDINARY DAY PLANNER

M T W TH F SA SU --- JAN. FEB. MAR. APR. MAY JUN. JUL. AUG. SEPT. OCT. NOV. DEC.

1 2 3 4 5 6 7 8 9 10 11 12 13 14 15 16 17 18 19 20 21 22 23 24 25 26 27 28 29 30 31

MY TOP 4 EXTRAORDINARY PRIORITIES

- [ ]
- [ ]
- [ ]
- [ ]

EXTRAORDINARY PEOPLE

- [ ]
- [ ]
- [ ]
- [ ]
- [ ]
- [ ]
- [ ]
- [ ]
- [ ]
- [ ]

MY EXTRAORDINARY TASKS

- [ ]
- [ ]
- [ ]
- [ ]

MY EXTRAORDINARY PROJECTS

- [ ]
- [ ]
- [ ]
- [ ]

MY EXTRAORDINARY HABITS

- [ ]
- [ ]
- [ ]
- [ ]

MY EXTRAORDINARY APPOINTMENTS

5:00 ______	3:00 ______
5:30 ______	3:30 ______
6:00 ______	4:00 ______
6:30 ______	4:30 ______
7:00 ______	5:00 ______
7:30 ______	5:30 ______
8:00 ______	6:00 ______
8:30 ______	6:30 ______
9:00 ______	7:00 ______
9:30 ______	7:30 ______
10:00 ______	8:00 ______
10:30 ______	8:30 ______
11:00 ______	9:00 ______
11:30 ______	9:30 ______
12:00 ______	10:00 ______
12:30 ______	10:30 ______
1:00 ______	11:00 ______
1:30 ______	11:30 ______
2:00 ______	12:00 ______
2:30 ______	12:30 ______

MY EXTRAORDINARY NOTES

MY EXTRAORDINARY DAY PLANNER

M T W TH F SA SU --- JAN. FEB. MAR. APR. MAY JUN. JUL. AUG. SEPT. OCT. NOV. DEC.

1 2 3 4 5 6 7 8 9 10 11 12 13 14 15 16 17 18 19 20 21 22 23 24 25 26 27 28 29 30 31

MY TOP 4 EXTRAORDINARY PRIORITIES

- [ ]
- [ ]
- [ ]
- [ ]

EXTRAORDINARY PEOPLE

- [ ]
- [ ]
- [ ]
- [ ]
- [ ]
- [ ]
- [ ]
- [ ]
- [ ]
- [ ]

MY EXTRAORDINARY TASKS

- [ ]
- [ ]
- [ ]
- [ ]

MY EXTRAORDINARY PROJECTS

- [ ]
- [ ]
- [ ]
- [ ]

MY EXTRAORDINARY HABITS

- [ ]
- [ ]
- [ ]
- [ ]

MY EXTRAORDINARY APPOINTMENTS

5:00 ____
5:30 ____
6:00 ____
6:30 ____
7:00 ____
7:30 ____
8:00 ____
8:30 ____
9:00 ____
9:30 ____
10:00 ____
10:30 ____
11:00 ____
11:30 ____
12:00 ____
12:30 ____
1:00 ____
1:30 ____
2:00 ____
2:30 ____

3:00 ____
3:30 ____
4:00 ____
4:30 ____
5:00 ____
5:30 ____
6:00 ____
6:30 ____
7:00 ____
7:30 ____
8:00 ____
8:30 ____
9:00 ____
9:30 ____
10:00 ____
10:30 ____
11:00 ____
11:30 ____
12:00 ____
12:30 ____

MY EXTRAORDINARY NOTES

MY EXTRAORDINARY DAY PLANNER

M T W TH F SA SU --- JAN. FEB. MAR. APR. MAY JUN. JUL. AUG. SEPT. OCT. NOV. DEC.

1 2 3 4 5 6 7 8 9 10 11 12 13 14 15 16 17 18 19 20 21 22 23 24 25 26 27 28 29 30 31

MY TOP 4 EXTRAORDINARY PRIORITIES

- [ ]
- [ ]
- [ ]
- [ ]

MY EXTRAORDINARY PROJECTS

- [ ]
- [ ]
- [ ]
- [ ]

EXTRAORDINARY PEOPLE

- [ ]
- [ ]
- [ ]
- [ ]
- [ ]
- [ ]
- [ ]
- [ ]
- [ ]
- [ ]

MY EXTRAORDINARY TASKS

- [ ]
- [ ]
- [ ]
- [ ]

MY EXTRAORDINARY HABITS

- [ ]
- [ ]
- [ ]
- [ ]

MY EXTRAORDINARY APPOINTMENTS

5:00 ______
5:30 ______
6:00 ______
6:30 ______
7:00 ______
7:30 ______
8:00 ______
8:30 ______
9:00 ______
9:30 ______
10:00 ______
10:30 ______
11:00 ______
11:30 ______
12:00 ______
12:30 ______
1:00 ______
1:30 ______
2:00 ______
2:30 ______
3:00 ______
3:30 ______
4:00 ______
4:30 ______
5:00 ______
5:30 ______
6:00 ______
6:30 ______
7:00 ______
7:30 ______
8:00 ______
8:30 ______
9:00 ______
9:30 ______
10:00 ______
10:30 ______
11:00 ______
11:30 ______
12:00 ______
12:30 ______

MY EXTRAORDINARY NOTES

MY EXTRAORDINARY 30-DAY REVIEW

Week of: ______________________________

Month of: _____________________________

The "WINS" for this past week/month were:

____

____

____

What I did not get done, but intended to do:

____

____

____

Challenges, situations, and/or problems I am facing now:

____

____

____

MY EXTRAORDINARY 30-DAY REVIEW

Opportunities I see for myself right now:

What I will do before the end of this coming week/month:

Notes:

MY EXTRAORDINARY DAY PLANNER

M T W TH F SA SU --- JAN. FEB. MAR. APR. MAY JUN. JUL. AUG. SEPT. OCT. NOV. DEC.

1 2 3 4 5 6 7 8 9 10 11 12 13 14 15 16 17 18 19 20 21 22 23 24 25 26 27 28 29 30 31

MY TOP 4 EXTRAORDINARY PRIORITIES

- ☐
- ☐
- ☐
- ☐

MY EXTRAORDINARY PROJECTS

- ☐
- ☐
- ☐
- ☐

EXTRAORDINARY PEOPLE

- ☐
- ☐
- ☐
- ☐
- ☐
- ☐
- ☐
- ☐
- ☐
- ☐

MY EXTRAORDINARY TASKS

- ☐
- ☐
- ☐
- ☐

MY EXTRAORDINARY HABITS

- ☐
- ☐
- ☐
- ☐

MY EXTRAORDINARY APPOINTMENTS

5:00 ____________________
5:30 ____________________
6:00 ____________________
6:30 ____________________
7:00 ____________________
7:30 ____________________
8:00 ____________________
8:30 ____________________
9:00 ____________________
9:30 ____________________
10:00 ____________________
10:30 ____________________
11:00 ____________________
11:30 ____________________
12:00 ____________________
12:30 ____________________
1:00 ____________________
1:30 ____________________
2:00 ____________________
2:30 ____________________

3:00 ____________________
3:30 ____________________
4:00 ____________________
4:30 ____________________
5:00 ____________________
5:30 ____________________
6:00 ____________________
6:30 ____________________
7:00 ____________________
7:30 ____________________
8:00 ____________________
8:30 ____________________
9:00 ____________________
9:30 ____________________
10:00 ____________________
10:30 ____________________
11:00 ____________________
11:30 ____________________
12:00 ____________________
12:30 ____________________

MY EXTRAORDINARY NOTES

MY EXTRAORDINARY DAY PLANNER

M T W TH F SA SU --- JAN. FEB. MAR. APR. MAY JUN. JUL. AUG. SEPT. OCT. NOV. DEC.

1 2 3 4 5 6 7 8 9 10 11 12 13 14 15 16 17 18 19 20 21 22 23 24 25 26 27 28 29 30 31

MY TOP 4 EXTRAORDINARY PRIORITIES

- [ ]
- [ ]
- [ ]
- [ ]

EXTRAORDINARY PEOPLE

- [ ]
- [ ]
- [ ]
- [ ]
- [ ]
- [ ]
- [ ]
- [ ]
- [ ]
- [ ]

MY EXTRAORDINARY TASKS

- [ ]
- [ ]
- [ ]
- [ ]

MY EXTRAORDINARY PROJECTS

- [ ]
- [ ]
- [ ]
- [ ]

MY EXTRAORDINARY HABITS

- [ ]
- [ ]
- [ ]
- [ ]

MY EXTRAORDINARY APPOINTMENTS

5:00 ______	3:00 ______
5:30 ______	3:30 ______
6:00 ______	4:00 ______
6:30 ______	4:30 ______
7:00 ______	5:00 ______
7:30 ______	5:30 ______
8:00 ______	6:00 ______
8:30 ______	6:30 ______
9:00 ______	7:00 ______
9:30 ______	7:30 ______
10:00 ______	8:00 ______
10:30 ______	8:30 ______
11:00 ______	9:00 ______
11:30 ______	9:30 ______
12:00 ______	10:00 ______
12:30 ______	10:30 ______
1:00 ______	11:00 ______
1:30 ______	11:30 ______
2:00 ______	12:00 ______
2:30 ______	12:30 ______

MY EXTRAORDINARY NOTES

MY EXTRAORDINARY DAY PLANNER

M T W TH F SA SU --- JAN. FEB. MAR. APR. MAY JUN. JUL. AUG. SEPT. OCT. NOV. DEC.

1 2 3 4 5 6 7 8 9 10 11 12 13 14 15 16 17 18 19 20 21 22 23 24 25 26 27 28 29 30 31

MY TOP 4 EXTRAORDINARY PRIORITIES

- ☐
- ☐
- ☐
- ☐

EXTRAORDINARY PEOPLE

- ☐
- ☐
- ☐
- ☐
- ☐
- ☐
- ☐
- ☐
- ☐
- ☐

MY EXTRAORDINARY TASKS

- ☐
- ☐
- ☐
- ☐

MY EXTRAORDINARY PROJECTS

- ☐
- ☐
- ☐
- ☐

MY EXTRAORDINARY HABITS

- ☐
- ☐
- ☐
- ☐

MY EXTRAORDINARY APPOINTMENTS

5:00		3:00	
5:30		3:30	
6:00		4:00	
6:30		4:30	
7:00		5:00	
7:30		5:30	
8:00		6:00	
8:30		6:30	
9:00		7:00	
9:30		7:30	
10:00		8:00	
10:30		8:30	
11:00		9:00	
11:30		9:30	
12:00		10:00	
12:30		10:30	
1:00		11:00	
1:30		11:30	
2:00		12:00	
2:30		12:30	

MY EXTRAORDINARY NOTES

MY EXTRAORDINARY DAY PLANNER

M T W TH F SA SU --- JAN. FEB. MAR. APR. MAY JUN. JUL. AUG. SEPT. OCT. NOV. DEC.

1 2 3 4 5 6 7 8 9 10 11 12 13 14 15 16 17 18 19 20 21 22 23 24 25 26 27 28 29 30 31

MY TOP 4 EXTRAORDINARY PRIORITIES

- ☐
- ☐
- ☐
- ☐

EXTRAORDINARY PEOPLE

- ☐
- ☐
- ☐
- ☐
- ☐
- ☐
- ☐
- ☐
- ☐
- ☐

MY EXTRAORDINARY TASKS

- ☐
- ☐
- ☐
- ☐

MY EXTRAORDINARY PROJECTS

- ☐
- ☐
- ☐
- ☐

MY EXTRAORDINARY HABITS

- ☐
- ☐
- ☐
- ☐

MY EXTRAORDINARY APPOINTMENTS

5:00 ____
5:30 ____
6:00 ____
6:30 ____
7:00 ____
7:30 ____
8:00 ____
8:30 ____
9:00 ____
9:30 ____
10:00 ____
10:30 ____
11:00 ____
11:30 ____
12:00 ____
12:30 ____
1:00 ____
1:30 ____
2:00 ____
2:30 ____

3:00 ____
3:30 ____
4:00 ____
4:30 ____
5:00 ____
5:30 ____
6:00 ____
6:30 ____
7:00 ____
7:30 ____
8:00 ____
8:30 ____
9:00 ____
9:30 ____
10:00 ____
10:30 ____
11:00 ____
11:30 ____
12:00 ____
12:30 ____

MY EXTRAORDINARY NOTES

MY EXTRAORDINARY DAY PLANNER

M T W TH F SA SU --- JAN. FEB. MAR. APR. MAY JUN. JUL. AUG. SEPT. OCT. NOV. DEC.

1 2 3 4 5 6 7 8 9 10 11 12 13 14 15 16 17 18 19 20 21 22 23 24 25 26 27 28 29 30 31

MY TOP 4 EXTRAORDINARY PRIORITIES

- [ ]
- [ ]
- [ ]
- [ ]

MY EXTRAORDINARY PROJECTS

- [ ]
- [ ]
- [ ]
- [ ]

EXTRAORDINARY PEOPLE

- [ ]
- [ ]
- [ ]
- [ ]
- [ ]
- [ ]
- [ ]
- [ ]
- [ ]
- [ ]

MY EXTRAORDINARY TASKS

- [ ]
- [ ]
- [ ]
- [ ]

MY EXTRAORDINARY HABITS

- [ ]
- [ ]
- [ ]
- [ ]

MY EXTRAORDINARY APPOINTMENTS

5:00 ____________________
5:30 ____________________
6:00 ____________________
6:30 ____________________
7:00 ____________________
7:30 ____________________
8:00 ____________________
8:30 ____________________
9:00 ____________________
9:30 ____________________
10:00 ____________________
10:30 ____________________
11:00 ____________________
11:30 ____________________
12:00 ____________________
12:30 ____________________
1:00 ____________________
1:30 ____________________
2:00 ____________________
2:30 ____________________

3:00 ____________________
3:30 ____________________
4:00 ____________________
4:30 ____________________
5:00 ____________________
5:30 ____________________
6:00 ____________________
6:30 ____________________
7:00 ____________________
7:30 ____________________
8:00 ____________________
8:30 ____________________
9:00 ____________________
9:30 ____________________
10:00 ____________________
10:30 ____________________
11:00 ____________________
11:30 ____________________
12:00 ____________________
12:30 ____________________

MY EXTRAORDINARY NOTES

MY EXTRAORDINARY DAY PLANNER

M T W TH F SA SU --- JAN. FEB. MAR. APR. MAY JUN. JUL. AUG. SEPT. OCT. NOV. DEC.

1 2 3 4 5 6 7 8 9 10 11 12 13 14 15 16 17 18 19 20 21 22 23 24 25 26 27 28 29 30 31

MY TOP 4 EXTRAORDINARY PRIORITIES

- [ ]
- [ ]
- [ ]
- [ ]

MY EXTRAORDINARY PROJECTS

- [ ]
- [ ]
- [ ]
- [ ]

EXTRAORDINARY PEOPLE

- [ ]
- [ ]
- [ ]
- [ ]
- [ ]
- [ ]
- [ ]
- [ ]
- [ ]
- [ ]

MY EXTRAORDINARY TASKS

- [ ]
- [ ]
- [ ]
- [ ]

MY EXTRAORDINARY HABITS

- [ ]
- [ ]
- [ ]
- [ ]

MY EXTRAORDINARY APPOINTMENTS

5:00 ______
5:30 ______
6:00 ______
6:30 ______
7:00 ______
7:30 ______
8:00 ______
8:30 ______
9:00 ______
9:30 ______
10:00 ______
10:30 ______
11:00 ______
11:30 ______
12:00 ______
12:30 ______
1:00 ______
1:30 ______
2:00 ______
2:30 ______
3:00 ______
3:30 ______
4:00 ______
4:30 ______
5:00 ______
5:30 ______
6:00 ______
6:30 ______
7:00 ______
7:30 ______
8:00 ______
8:30 ______
9:00 ______
9:30 ______
10:00 ______
10:30 ______
11:00 ______
11:30 ______
12:00 ______
12:30 ______

MY EXTRAORDINARY NOTES

MY EXTRAORDINARY DAY PLANNER

M T W TH F SA SU --- JAN. FEB. MAR. APR. MAY JUN. JUL. AUG. SEPT. OCT. NOV. DEC.

1 2 3 4 5 6 7 8 9 10 11 12 13 14 15 16 17 18 19 20 21 22 23 24 25 26 27 28 29 30 31

MY TOP 4 EXTRAORDINARY PRIORITIES

- [ ]
- [ ]
- [ ]
- [ ]

EXTRAORDINARY PEOPLE

- [ ]
- [ ]
- [ ]
- [ ]
- [ ]
- [ ]
- [ ]
- [ ]
- [ ]
- [ ]

MY EXTRAORDINARY TASKS

- [ ]
- [ ]
- [ ]
- [ ]

MY EXTRAORDINARY PROJECTS

- [ ]
- [ ]
- [ ]
- [ ]

MY EXTRAORDINARY HABITS

- [ ]
- [ ]
- [ ]
- [ ]

MY EXTRAORDINARY APPOINTMENTS

5:00 ____
5:30 ____
6:00 ____
6:30 ____
7:00 ____
7:30 ____
8:00 ____
8:30 ____
9:00 ____
9:30 ____
10:00 ____
10:30 ____
11:00 ____
11:30 ____
12:00 ____
12:30 ____
1:00 ____
1:30 ____
2:00 ____
2:30 ____
3:00 ____
3:30 ____
4:00 ____
4:30 ____
5:00 ____
5:30 ____
6:00 ____
6:30 ____
7:00 ____
7:30 ____
8:00 ____
8:30 ____
9:00 ____
9:30 ____
10:00 ____
10:30 ____
11:00 ____
11:30 ____
12:00 ____
12:30 ____

MY EXTRAORDINARY NOTES

MY EXTRAORDINARY DAY PLANNER

M T W TH F SA SU --- JAN. FEB. MAR. APR. MAY JUN. JUL. AUG. SEPT. OCT. NOV. DEC.

1 2 3 4 5 6 7 8 9 10 11 12 13 14 15 16 17 18 19 20 21 22 23 24 25 26 27 28 29 30 31

MY TOP 4 EXTRAORDINARY PRIORITIES

- [ ]
- [ ]
- [ ]
- [ ]

EXTRAORDINARY PEOPLE

- [ ]
- [ ]
- [ ]
- [ ]
- [ ]
- [ ]
- [ ]
- [ ]
- [ ]
- [ ]

MY EXTRAORDINARY TASKS

- [ ]
- [ ]
- [ ]
- [ ]

MY EXTRAORDINARY PROJECTS

- [ ]
- [ ]
- [ ]
- [ ]

MY EXTRAORDINARY HABITS

- [ ]
- [ ]
- [ ]
- [ ]

MY EXTRAORDINARY APPOINTMENTS

5:00 ____
5:30 ____
6:00 ____
6:30 ____
7:00 ____
7:30 ____
8:00 ____
8:30 ____
9:00 ____
9:30 ____
10:00 ____
10:30 ____
11:00 ____
11:30 ____
12:00 ____
12:30 ____
1:00 ____
1:30 ____
2:00 ____
2:30 ____
3:00 ____
3:30 ____
4:00 ____
4:30 ____
5:00 ____
5:30 ____
6:00 ____
6:30 ____
7:00 ____
7:30 ____
8:00 ____
8:30 ____
9:00 ____
9:30 ____
10:00 ____
10:30 ____
11:00 ____
11:30 ____
12:00 ____
12:30 ____

MY EXTRAORDINARY NOTES

MY EXTRAORDINARY DAY PLANNER

M T W TH F SA SU --- JAN. FEB. MAR. APR. MAY JUN. JUL. AUG. SEPT. OCT. NOV. DEC.

1 2 3 4 5 6 7 8 9 10 11 12 13 14 15 16 17 18 19 20 21 22 23 24 25 26 27 28 29 30 31

MY TOP 4 EXTRAORDINARY PRIORITIES

- [ ]
- [ ]
- [ ]
- [ ]

EXTRAORDINARY PEOPLE

- [ ]
- [ ]
- [ ]
- [ ]
- [ ]
- [ ]
- [ ]
- [ ]
- [ ]
- [ ]

MY EXTRAORDINARY TASKS

- [ ]
- [ ]
- [ ]
- [ ]

MY EXTRAORDINARY PROJECTS

- [ ]
- [ ]
- [ ]
- [ ]

MY EXTRAORDINARY HABITS

- [ ]
- [ ]
- [ ]
- [ ]

MY EXTRAORDINARY APPOINTMENTS

5:00		3:00	
5:30		3:30	
6:00		4:00	
6:30		4:30	
7:00		5:00	
7:30		5:30	
8:00		6:00	
8:30		6:30	
9:00		7:00	
9:30		7:30	
10:00		8:00	
10:30		8:30	
11:00		9:00	
11:30		9:30	
12:00		10:00	
12:30		10:30	
1:00		11:00	
1:30		11:30	
2:00		12:00	
2:30		12:30	

MY EXTRAORDINARY NOTES

MY EXTRAORDINARY DAY PLANNER

M T W TH F SA SU --- JAN. FEB. MAR. APR. MAY JUN. JUL. AUG. SEPT. OCT. NOV. DEC.

1 2 3 4 5 6 7 8 9 10 11 12 13 14 15 16 17 18 19 20 21 22 23 24 25 26 27 28 29 30 31

MY TOP 4 EXTRAORDINARY PRIORITIES

- ☐
- ☐
- ☐
- ☐

EXTRAORDINARY PEOPLE

- ☐
- ☐
- ☐
- ☐
- ☐
- ☐
- ☐
- ☐
- ☐
- ☐

MY EXTRAORDINARY TASKS

- ☐
- ☐
- ☐
- ☐

MY EXTRAORDINARY PROJECTS

- ☐
- ☐
- ☐
- ☐

MY EXTRAORDINARY HABITS

- ☐
- ☐
- ☐
- ☐

MY EXTRAORDINARY APPOINTMENTS

5:00		3:00	
5:30		3:30	
6:00		4:00	
6:30		4:30	
7:00		5:00	
7:30		5:30	
8:00		6:00	
8:30		6:30	
9:00		7:00	
9:30		7:30	
10:00		8:00	
10:30		8:30	
11:00		9:00	
11:30		9:30	
12:00		10:00	
12:30		10:30	
1:00		11:00	
1:30		11:30	
2:00		12:00	
2:30		12:30	

MY EXTRAORDINARY NOTES

MY EXTRAORDINARY DAY PLANNER

M T W TH F SA SU --- JAN. FEB. MAR. APR. MAY JUN. JUL. AUG. SEPT. OCT. NOV. DEC.

1 2 3 4 5 6 7 8 9 10 11 12 13 14 15 16 17 18 19 20 21 22 23 24 25 26 27 28 29 30 31

MY TOP 4 EXTRAORDINARY PRIORITIES

- [ ]
- [ ]
- [ ]
- [ ]

EXTRAORDINARY PEOPLE

- [ ]
- [ ]
- [ ]
- [ ]
- [ ]
- [ ]
- [ ]
- [ ]
- [ ]
- [ ]

MY EXTRAORDINARY TASKS

- [ ]
- [ ]
- [ ]
- [ ]

MY EXTRAORDINARY PROJECTS

- [ ]
- [ ]
- [ ]
- [ ]

MY EXTRAORDINARY HABITS

- [ ]
- [ ]
- [ ]
- [ ]

MY EXTRAORDINARY APPOINTMENTS

5:00		3:00	
5:30		3:30	
6:00		4:00	
6:30		4:30	
7:00		5:00	
7:30		5:30	
8:00		6:00	
8:30		6:30	
9:00		7:00	
9:30		7:30	
10:00		8:00	
10:30		8:30	
11:00		9:00	
11:30		9:30	
12:00		10:00	
12:30		10:30	
1:00		11:00	
1:30		11:30	
2:00		12:00	
2:30		12:30	

MY EXTRAORDINARY NOTES

MY EXTRAORDINARY DAY PLANNER

M T W TH F SA SU --- JAN. FEB. MAR. APR. MAY JUN. JUL. AUG. SEPT. OCT. NOV. DEC.

1 2 3 4 5 6 7 8 9 10 11 12 13 14 15 16 17 18 19 20 21 22 23 24 25 26 27 28 29 30 31

MY TOP 4 EXTRAORDINARY PRIORITIES

- [ ]
- [ ]
- [ ]
- [ ]

EXTRAORDINARY PEOPLE

- [ ]
- [ ]
- [ ]
- [ ]
- [ ]
- [ ]
- [ ]
- [ ]
- [ ]
- [ ]

MY EXTRAORDINARY TASKS

- [ ]
- [ ]
- [ ]
- [ ]

MY EXTRAORDINARY PROJECTS

- [ ]
- [ ]
- [ ]
- [ ]

MY EXTRAORDINARY HABITS

- [ ]
- [ ]
- [ ]
- [ ]

MY EXTRAORDINARY APPOINTMENTS

5:00 ______
5:30 ______
6:00 ______
6:30 ______
7:00 ______
7:30 ______
8:00 ______
8:30 ______
9:00 ______
9:30 ______
10:00 ______
10:30 ______
11:00 ______
11:30 ______
12:00 ______
12:30 ______
1:00 ______
1:30 ______
2:00 ______
2:30 ______
3:00 ______
3:30 ______
4:00 ______
4:30 ______
5:00 ______
5:30 ______
6:00 ______
6:30 ______
7:00 ______
7:30 ______
8:00 ______
8:30 ______
9:00 ______
9:30 ______
10:00 ______
10:30 ______
11:00 ______
11:30 ______
12:00 ______
12:30 ______

MY EXTRAORDINARY NOTES

MY EXTRAORDINARY DAY PLANNER

M T W TH F SA SU --- JAN. FEB. MAR. APR. MAY JUN. JUL. AUG. SEPT. OCT. NOV. DEC.

1 2 3 4 5 6 7 8 9 10 11 12 13 14 15 16 17 18 19 20 21 22 23 24 25 26 27 28 29 30 31

MY TOP 4 EXTRAORDINARY PRIORITIES

- ☐
- ☐
- ☐
- ☐

EXTRAORDINARY PEOPLE

- ☐
- ☐
- ☐
- ☐
- ☐
- ☐
- ☐
- ☐
- ☐
- ☐

MY EXTRAORDINARY TASKS

- ☐
- ☐
- ☐
- ☐

MY EXTRAORDINARY PROJECTS

- ☐
- ☐
- ☐
- ☐

MY EXTRAORDINARY HABITS

- ☐
- ☐
- ☐
- ☐

MY EXTRAORDINARY APPOINTMENTS

5:00 __________
5:30 __________
6:00 __________
6:30 __________
7:00 __________
7:30 __________
8:00 __________
8:30 __________
9:00 __________
9:30 __________
10:00 __________
10:30 __________
11:00 __________
11:30 __________
12:00 __________
12:30 __________
1:00 __________
1:30 __________
2:00 __________
2:30 __________
3:00 __________
3:30 __________
4:00 __________
4:30 __________
5:00 __________
5:30 __________
6:00 __________
6:30 __________
7:00 __________
7:30 __________
8:00 __________
8:30 __________
9:00 __________
9:30 __________
10:00 __________
10:30 __________
11:00 __________
11:30 __________
12:00 __________
12:30 __________

MY EXTRAORDINARY NOTES

MY EXTRAORDINARY DAY PLANNER

M T W TH F SA SU --- JAN. FEB. MAR. APR. MAY JUN. JUL. AUG. SEPT. OCT. NOV. DEC.

1 2 3 4 5 6 7 8 9 10 11 12 13 14 15 16 17 18 19 20 21 22 23 24 25 26 27 28 29 30 31

MY TOP 4 EXTRAORDINARY PRIORITIES

- [ ]
- [ ]
- [ ]
- [ ]

EXTRAORDINARY PEOPLE

- [ ]
- [ ]
- [ ]
- [ ]
- [ ]
- [ ]
- [ ]
- [ ]
- [ ]
- [ ]

MY EXTRAORDINARY TASKS

- [ ]
- [ ]
- [ ]
- [ ]

MY EXTRAORDINARY PROJECTS

- [ ]
- [ ]
- [ ]
- [ ]

MY EXTRAORDINARY HABITS

- [ ]
- [ ]
- [ ]
- [ ]

MY EXTRAORDINARY APPOINTMENTS

5:00 __________
5:30 __________
6:00 __________
6:30 __________
7:00 __________
7:30 __________
8:00 __________
8:30 __________
9:00 __________
9:30 __________
10:00 __________
10:30 __________
11:00 __________
11:30 __________
12:00 __________
12:30 __________
1:00 __________
1:30 __________
2:00 __________
2:30 __________
3:00 __________
3:30 __________
4:00 __________
4:30 __________
5:00 __________
5:30 __________
6:00 __________
6:30 __________
7:00 __________
7:30 __________
8:00 __________
8:30 __________
9:00 __________
9:30 __________
10:00 __________
10:30 __________
11:00 __________
11:30 __________
12:00 __________
12:30 __________

MY EXTRAORDINARY NOTES

MY EXTRAORDINARY DAY PLANNER

M T W TH F SA SU --- JAN. FEB. MAR. APR. MAY JUN. JUL. AUG. SEPT. OCT. NOV. DEC.

1 2 3 4 5 6 7 8 9 10 11 12 13 14 15 16 17 18 19 20 21 22 23 24 25 26 27 28 29 30 31

MY TOP 4 EXTRAORDINARY PRIORITIES

- [ ]
- [ ]
- [ ]
- [ ]

EXTRAORDINARY PEOPLE

- [ ]
- [ ]
- [ ]
- [ ]
- [ ]
- [ ]
- [ ]
- [ ]
- [ ]
- [ ]

MY EXTRAORDINARY TASKS

- [ ]
- [ ]
- [ ]
- [ ]

MY EXTRAORDINARY PROJECTS

- [ ]
- [ ]
- [ ]
- [ ]

MY EXTRAORDINARY HABITS

- [ ]
- [ ]
- [ ]
- [ ]

MY EXTRAORDINARY APPOINTMENTS

5:00 ____
5:30 ____
6:00 ____
6:30 ____
7:00 ____
7:30 ____
8:00 ____
8:30 ____
9:00 ____
9:30 ____
10:00 ____
10:30 ____
11:00 ____
11:30 ____
12:00 ____
12:30 ____
1:00 ____
1:30 ____
2:00 ____
2:30 ____
3:00 ____
3:30 ____
4:00 ____
4:30 ____
5:00 ____
5:30 ____
6:00 ____
6:30 ____
7:00 ____
7:30 ____
8:00 ____
8:30 ____
9:00 ____
9:30 ____
10:00 ____
10:30 ____
11:00 ____
11:30 ____
12:00 ____
12:30 ____

MY EXTRAORDINARY NOTES

MY EXTRAORDINARY DAY PLANNER

M T W TH F SA SU --- JAN. FEB. MAR. APR. MAY JUN. JUL. AUG. SEPT. OCT. NOV. DEC.

1 2 3 4 5 6 7 8 9 10 11 12 13 14 15 16 17 18 19 20 21 22 23 24 25 26 27 28 29 30 31

MY TOP 4 EXTRAORDINARY PRIORITIES

- [ ]
- [ ]
- [ ]
- [ ]

EXTRAORDINARY PEOPLE

- [ ]
- [ ]
- [ ]
- [ ]
- [ ]
- [ ]
- [ ]
- [ ]
- [ ]
- [ ]

MY EXTRAORDINARY TASKS

- [ ]
- [ ]
- [ ]
- [ ]

MY EXTRAORDINARY PROJECTS

- [ ]
- [ ]
- [ ]
- [ ]

MY EXTRAORDINARY HABITS

- [ ]
- [ ]
- [ ]
- [ ]

MY EXTRAORDINARY APPOINTMENTS

5:00 ________
5:30 ________
6:00 ________
6:30 ________
7:00 ________
7:30 ________
8:00 ________
8:30 ________
9:00 ________
9:30 ________
10:00 ________
10:30 ________
11:00 ________
11:30 ________
12:00 ________
12:30 ________
1:00 ________
1:30 ________
2:00 ________
2:30 ________
3:00 ________
3:30 ________
4:00 ________
4:30 ________
5:00 ________
5:30 ________
6:00 ________
6:30 ________
7:00 ________
7:30 ________
8:00 ________
8:30 ________
9:00 ________
9:30 ________
10:00 ________
10:30 ________
11:00 ________
11:30 ________
12:00 ________
12:30 ________

MY EXTRAORDINARY NOTES

MY EXTRAORDINARY DAY PLANNER

M T W TH F SA SU --- JAN. FEB. MAR. APR. MAY JUN. JUL. AUG. SEPT. OCT. NOV. DEC.

1 2 3 4 5 6 7 8 9 10 11 12 13 14 15 16 17 18 19 20 21 22 23 24 25 26 27 28 29 30 31

MY TOP 4 EXTRAORDINARY PRIORITIES

☐
☐
☐
☐

EXTRAORDINARY PEOPLE

☐
☐
☐
☐
☐
☐
☐
☐
☐
☐

MY EXTRAORDINARY TASKS

☐
☐
☐
☐

MY EXTRAORDINARY PROJECTS

☐
☐
☐
☐

MY EXTRAORDINARY HABITS

☐
☐
☐
☐

MY EXTRAORDINARY APPOINTMENTS

5:00 ____
5:30 ____
6:00 ____
6:30 ____
7:00 ____
7:30 ____
8:00 ____
8:30 ____
9:00 ____
9:30 ____
10:00 ____
10:30 ____
11:00 ____
11:30 ____
12:00 ____
12:30 ____
1:00 ____
1:30 ____
2:00 ____
2:30 ____
3:00 ____
3:30 ____
4:00 ____
4:30 ____
5:00 ____
5:30 ____
6:00 ____
6:30 ____
7:00 ____
7:30 ____
8:00 ____
8:30 ____
9:00 ____
9:30 ____
10:00 ____
10:30 ____
11:00 ____
11:30 ____
12:00 ____
12:30 ____

MY EXTRAORDINARY NOTES

MY EXTRAORDINARY DAY PLANNER

M T W TH F SA SU --- JAN. FEB. MAR. APR. MAY JUN. JUL. AUG. SEPT. OCT. NOV. DEC.

1 2 3 4 5 6 7 8 9 10 11 12 13 14 15 16 17 18 19 20 21 22 23 24 25 26 27 28 29 30 31

MY TOP 4 EXTRAORDINARY PRIORITIES

- [ ]
- [ ]
- [ ]
- [ ]

EXTRAORDINARY PEOPLE

- [ ]
- [ ]
- [ ]
- [ ]
- [ ]
- [ ]
- [ ]
- [ ]
- [ ]
- [ ]

MY EXTRAORDINARY TASKS

- [ ]
- [ ]
- [ ]
- [ ]

MY EXTRAORDINARY PROJECTS

- [ ]
- [ ]
- [ ]
- [ ]

MY EXTRAORDINARY HABITS

- [ ]
- [ ]
- [ ]
- [ ]

MY EXTRAORDINARY APPOINTMENTS

5:00 ______
5:30 ______
6:00 ______
6:30 ______
7:00 ______
7:30 ______
8:00 ______
8:30 ______
9:00 ______
9:30 ______
10:00 ______
10:30 ______
11:00 ______
11:30 ______
12:00 ______
12:30 ______
1:00 ______
1:30 ______
2:00 ______
2:30 ______
3:00 ______
3:30 ______
4:00 ______
4:30 ______
5:00 ______
5:30 ______
6:00 ______
6:30 ______
7:00 ______
7:30 ______
8:00 ______
8:30 ______
9:00 ______
9:30 ______
10:00 ______
10:30 ______
11:00 ______
11:30 ______
12:00 ______
12:30 ______

MY EXTRAORDINARY NOTES

MY EXTRAORDINARY DAY PLANNER

M T W TH F SA SU --- JAN. FEB. MAR. APR. MAY JUN. JUL. AUG. SEPT. OCT. NOV. DEC.

1 2 3 4 5 6 7 8 9 10 11 12 13 14 15 16 17 18 19 20 21 22 23 24 25 26 27 28 29 30 31

MY TOP 4 EXTRAORDINARY PRIORITIES

- ☐
- ☐
- ☐
- ☐

EXTRAORDINARY PEOPLE

- ☐
- ☐
- ☐
- ☐
- ☐
- ☐
- ☐
- ☐
- ☐
- ☐

MY EXTRAORDINARY TASKS

- ☐
- ☐
- ☐
- ☐

MY EXTRAORDINARY PROJECTS

- ☐
- ☐
- ☐
- ☐

MY EXTRAORDINARY HABITS

- ☐
- ☐
- ☐
- ☐

MY EXTRAORDINARY APPOINTMENTS

5:00 __________
5:30 __________
6:00 __________
6:30 __________
7:00 __________
7:30 __________
8:00 __________
8:30 __________
9:00 __________
9:30 __________
10:00 __________
10:30 __________
11:00 __________
11:30 __________
12:00 __________
12:30 __________
1:00 __________
1:30 __________
2:00 __________
2:30 __________
3:00 __________
3:30 __________
4:00 __________
4:30 __________
5:00 __________
5:30 __________
6:00 __________
6:30 __________
7:00 __________
7:30 __________
8:00 __________
8:30 __________
9:00 __________
9:30 __________
10:00 __________
10:30 __________
11:00 __________
11:30 __________
12:00 __________
12:30 __________

MY EXTRAORDINARY NOTES

MY EXTRAORDINARY DAY PLANNER

M T W TH F SA SU --- JAN. FEB. MAR. APR. MAY JUN. JUL. AUG. SEPT. OCT. NOV. DEC.

1 2 3 4 5 6 7 8 9 10 11 12 13 14 15 16 17 18 19 20 21 22 23 24 25 26 27 28 29 30 31

MY TOP 4 EXTRAORDINARY PRIORITIES

☐
☐
☐
☐

EXTRAORDINARY PEOPLE

☐
☐
☐
☐
☐
☐
☐
☐
☐
☐

MY EXTRAORDINARY TASKS

☐
☐
☐
☐

MY EXTRAORDINARY PROJECTS

☐
☐
☐
☐

MY EXTRAORDINARY HABITS

☐
☐
☐
☐

MY EXTRAORDINARY APPOINTMENTS

5:00 ________
5:30 ________
6:00 ________
6:30 ________
7:00 ________
7:30 ________
8:00 ________
8:30 ________
9:00 ________
9:30 ________
10:00 ________
10:30 ________
11:00 ________
11:30 ________
12:00 ________
12:30 ________
1:00 ________
1:30 ________
2:00 ________
2:30 ________
3:00 ________
3:30 ________
4:00 ________
4:30 ________
5:00 ________
5:30 ________
6:00 ________
6:30 ________
7:00 ________
7:30 ________
8:00 ________
8:30 ________
9:00 ________
9:30 ________
10:00 ________
10:30 ________
11:00 ________
11:30 ________
12:00 ________
12:30 ________

MY EXTRAORDINARY NOTES

MY EXTRAORDINARY DAY PLANNER

M T W TH F SA SU --- JAN. FEB. MAR. APR. MAY JUN. JUL. AUG. SEPT. OCT. NOV. DEC.

1 2 3 4 5 6 7 8 9 10 11 12 13 14 15 16 17 18 19 20 21 22 23 24 25 26 27 28 29 30 31

MY TOP 4 EXTRAORDINARY PRIORITIES

☐
☐
☐
☐

EXTRAORDINARY PEOPLE

☐
☐
☐
☐
☐
☐
☐
☐
☐
☐

MY EXTRAORDINARY TASKS

☐
☐
☐
☐

MY EXTRAORDINARY PROJECTS

☐
☐
☐
☐

MY EXTRAORDINARY HABITS

☐
☐
☐
☐

MY EXTRAORDINARY APPOINTMENTS

5:00 ______	3:00 ______
5:30 ______	3:30 ______
6:00 ______	4:00 ______
6:30 ______	4:30 ______
7:00 ______	5:00 ______
7:30 ______	5:30 ______
8:00 ______	6:00 ______
8:30 ______	6:30 ______
9:00 ______	7:00 ______
9:30 ______	7:30 ______
10:00 ______	8:00 ______
10:30 ______	8:30 ______
11:00 ______	9:00 ______
11:30 ______	9:30 ______
12:00 ______	10:00 ______
12:30 ______	10:30 ______
1:00 ______	11:00 ______
1:30 ______	11:30 ______
2:00 ______	12:00 ______
2:30 ______	12:30 ______

MY EXTRAORDINARY NOTES

MY EXTRAORDINARY DAY PLANNER

M T W TH F SA SU --- JAN. FEB. MAR. APR. MAY JUN. JUL. AUG. SEPT. OCT. NOV. DEC.

1 2 3 4 5 6 7 8 9 10 11 12 13 14 15 16 17 18 19 20 21 22 23 24 25 26 27 28 29 30 31

MY TOP 4 EXTRAORDINARY PRIORITIES

☐
☐
☐
☐

EXTRAORDINARY PEOPLE

☐
☐
☐
☐
☐
☐
☐
☐
☐
☐

MY EXTRAORDINARY TASKS

☐
☐
☐
☐

MY EXTRAORDINARY PROJECTS

☐
☐
☐
☐

MY EXTRAORDINARY HABITS

☐
☐
☐
☐

MY EXTRAORDINARY APPOINTMENTS

5:00 ______	3:00 ______
5:30 ______	3:30 ______
6:00 ______	4:00 ______
6:30 ______	4:30 ______
7:00 ______	5:00 ______
7:30 ______	5:30 ______
8:00 ______	6:00 ______
8:30 ______	6:30 ______
9:00 ______	7:00 ______
9:30 ______	7:30 ______
10:00 ______	8:00 ______
10:30 ______	8:30 ______
11:00 ______	9:00 ______
11:30 ______	9:30 ______
12:00 ______	10:00 ______
12:30 ______	10:30 ______
1:00 ______	11:00 ______
1:30 ______	11:30 ______
2:00 ______	12:00 ______
2:30 ______	12:30 ______

MY EXTRAORDINARY NOTES

MY EXTRAORDINARY DAY PLANNER

M T W TH F SA SU --- JAN. FEB. MAR. APR. MAY JUN. JUL. AUG. SEPT. OCT. NOV. DEC.

1 2 3 4 5 6 7 8 9 10 11 12 13 14 15 16 17 18 19 20 21 22 23 24 25 26 27 28 29 30 31

MY TOP 4 EXTRAORDINARY PRIORITIES

- [ ]
- [ ]
- [ ]
- [ ]

EXTRAORDINARY PEOPLE

- [ ]
- [ ]
- [ ]
- [ ]
- [ ]
- [ ]
- [ ]
- [ ]
- [ ]
- [ ]

MY EXTRAORDINARY TASKS

- [ ]
- [ ]
- [ ]
- [ ]

MY EXTRAORDINARY PROJECTS

- [ ]
- [ ]
- [ ]
- [ ]

MY EXTRAORDINARY HABITS

- [ ]
- [ ]
- [ ]
- [ ]

MY EXTRAORDINARY APPOINTMENTS

5:00	3:00
5:30	3:30
6:00	4:00
6:30	4:30
7:00	5:00
7:30	5:30
8:00	6:00
8:30	6:30
9:00	7:00
9:30	7:30
10:00	8:00
10:30	8:30
11:00	9:00
11:30	9:30
12:00	10:00
12:30	10:30
1:00	11:00
1:30	11:30
2:00	12:00
2:30	12:30

MY EXTRAORDINARY NOTES

MY EXTRAORDINARY DAY PLANNER

M T W TH F SA SU --- JAN. FEB. MAR. APR. MAY JUN. JUL. AUG. SEPT. OCT. NOV. DEC.

1 2 3 4 5 6 7 8 9 10 11 12 13 14 15 16 17 18 19 20 21 22 23 24 25 26 27 28 29 30 31

MY TOP 4 EXTRAORDINARY PRIORITIES

- [ ]
- [ ]
- [ ]
- [ ]

EXTRAORDINARY PEOPLE

- [ ]
- [ ]
- [ ]
- [ ]
- [ ]
- [ ]
- [ ]
- [ ]
- [ ]
- [ ]

MY EXTRAORDINARY TASKS

- [ ]
- [ ]
- [ ]
- [ ]

MY EXTRAORDINARY PROJECTS

- [ ]
- [ ]
- [ ]
- [ ]

MY EXTRAORDINARY HABITS

- [ ]
- [ ]
- [ ]
- [ ]

MY EXTRAORDINARY APPOINTMENTS

5:00 ______
5:30 ______
6:00 ______
6:30 ______
7:00 ______
7:30 ______
8:00 ______
8:30 ______
9:00 ______
9:30 ______
10:00 ______
10:30 ______
11:00 ______
11:30 ______
12:00 ______
12:30 ______
1:00 ______
1:30 ______
2:00 ______
2:30 ______

3:00 ______
3:30 ______
4:00 ______
4:30 ______
5:00 ______
5:30 ______
6:00 ______
6:30 ______
7:00 ______
7:30 ______
8:00 ______
8:30 ______
9:00 ______
9:30 ______
10:00 ______
10:30 ______
11:00 ______
11:30 ______
12:00 ______
12:30 ______

MY EXTRAORDINARY NOTES

MY EXTRAORDINARY DAY PLANNER

M T W TH F SA SU --- JAN. FEB. MAR. APR. MAY JUN. JUL. AUG. SEPT. OCT. NOV. DEC.

1 2 3 4 5 6 7 8 9 10 11 12 13 14 15 16 17 18 19 20 21 22 23 24 25 26 27 28 29 30 31

MY TOP 4 EXTRAORDINARY PRIORITIES

- [ ]
- [ ]
- [ ]
- [ ]

EXTRAORDINARY PEOPLE

- [ ]
- [ ]
- [ ]
- [ ]
- [ ]
- [ ]
- [ ]
- [ ]
- [ ]
- [ ]

MY EXTRAORDINARY TASKS

- [ ]
- [ ]
- [ ]
- [ ]

MY EXTRAORDINARY PROJECTS

- [ ]
- [ ]
- [ ]
- [ ]

MY EXTRAORDINARY HABITS

- [ ]
- [ ]
- [ ]
- [ ]

MY EXTRAORDINARY APPOINTMENTS

5:00 ______
5:30 ______
6:00 ______
6:30 ______
7:00 ______
7:30 ______
8:00 ______
8:30 ______
9:00 ______
9:30 ______
10:00 ______
10:30 ______
11:00 ______
11:30 ______
12:00 ______
12:30 ______
1:00 ______
1:30 ______
2:00 ______
2:30 ______

3:00 ______
3:30 ______
4:00 ______
4:30 ______
5:00 ______
5:30 ______
6:00 ______
6:30 ______
7:00 ______
7:30 ______
8:00 ______
8:30 ______
9:00 ______
9:30 ______
10:00 ______
10:30 ______
11:00 ______
11:30 ______
12:00 ______
12:30 ______

MY EXTRAORDINARY NOTES

MY EXTRAORDINARY DAY PLANNER

M T W TH F SA SU --- JAN. FEB. MAR. APR. MAY JUN. JUL. AUG. SEPT. OCT. NOV. DEC.

1 2 3 4 5 6 7 8 9 10 11 12 13 14 15 16 17 18 19 20 21 22 23 24 25 26 27 28 29 30 31

MY TOP 4 EXTRAORDINARY PRIORITIES

- [ ]
- [ ]
- [ ]
- [ ]

EXTRAORDINARY PEOPLE

- [ ]
- [ ]
- [ ]
- [ ]
- [ ]
- [ ]
- [ ]
- [ ]
- [ ]
- [ ]

MY EXTRAORDINARY TASKS

- [ ]
- [ ]
- [ ]
- [ ]

MY EXTRAORDINARY PROJECTS

- [ ]
- [ ]
- [ ]
- [ ]

MY EXTRAORDINARY HABITS

- [ ]
- [ ]
- [ ]
- [ ]

MY EXTRAORDINARY APPOINTMENTS

5:00	3:00
5:30	3:30
6:00	4:00
6:30	4:30
7:00	5:00
7:30	5:30
8:00	6:00
8:30	6:30
9:00	7:00
9:30	7:30
10:00	8:00
10:30	8:30
11:00	9:00
11:30	9:30
12:00	10:00
12:30	10:30
1:00	11:00
1:30	11:30
2:00	12:00
2:30	12:30

MY EXTRAORDINARY NOTES

MY EXTRAORDINARY DAY PLANNER

M T W TH F SA SU --- JAN. FEB. MAR. APR. MAY JUN. JUL. AUG. SEPT. OCT. NOV. DEC.

1 2 3 4 5 6 7 8 9 10 11 12 13 14 15 16 17 18 19 20 21 22 23 24 25 26 27 28 29 30 31

MY TOP 4 EXTRAORDINARY PRIORITIES

- [ ]
- [ ]
- [ ]
- [ ]

EXTRAORDINARY PEOPLE

- [ ]
- [ ]
- [ ]
- [ ]
- [ ]
- [ ]
- [ ]
- [ ]
- [ ]
- [ ]

MY EXTRAORDINARY TASKS

- [ ]
- [ ]
- [ ]
- [ ]

MY EXTRAORDINARY PROJECTS

- [ ]
- [ ]
- [ ]
- [ ]

MY EXTRAORDINARY HABITS

- [ ]
- [ ]
- [ ]
- [ ]

MY EXTRAORDINARY APPOINTMENTS

5:00 ____
5:30 ____
6:00 ____
6:30 ____
7:00 ____
7:30 ____
8:00 ____
8:30 ____
9:00 ____
9:30 ____
10:00 ____
10:30 ____
11:00 ____
11:30 ____
12:00 ____
12:30 ____
1:00 ____
1:30 ____
2:00 ____
2:30 ____
3:00 ____
3:30 ____
4:00 ____
4:30 ____
5:00 ____
5:30 ____
6:00 ____
6:30 ____
7:00 ____
7:30 ____
8:00 ____
8:30 ____
9:00 ____
9:30 ____
10:00 ____
10:30 ____
11:00 ____
11:30 ____
12:00 ____
12:30 ____

MY EXTRAORDINARY NOTES

MY EXTRAORDINARY DAY PLANNER

M T W TH F SA SU --- JAN. FEB. MAR. APR. MAY JUN. JUL. AUG. SEPT. OCT. NOV. DEC.

1 2 3 4 5 6 7 8 9 10 11 12 13 14 15 16 17 18 19 20 21 22 23 24 25 26 27 28 29 30 31

MY TOP 4 EXTRAORDINARY PRIORITIES

- [ ]
- [ ]
- [ ]
- [ ]

MY EXTRAORDINARY PROJECTS

- [ ]
- [ ]
- [ ]
- [ ]

EXTRAORDINARY PEOPLE

- [ ]
- [ ]
- [ ]
- [ ]
- [ ]
- [ ]
- [ ]
- [ ]
- [ ]
- [ ]

MY EXTRAORDINARY TASKS

- [ ]
- [ ]
- [ ]
- [ ]

MY EXTRAORDINARY HABITS

- [ ]
- [ ]
- [ ]
- [ ]

MY EXTRAORDINARY APPOINTMENTS

5:00 ______
5:30 ______
6:00 ______
6:30 ______
7:00 ______
7:30 ______
8:00 ______
8:30 ______
9:00 ______
9:30 ______
10:00 ______
10:30 ______
11:00 ______
11:30 ______
12:00 ______
12:30 ______
1:00 ______
1:30 ______
2:00 ______
2:30 ______

3:00 ______
3:30 ______
4:00 ______
4:30 ______
5:00 ______
5:30 ______
6:00 ______
6:30 ______
7:00 ______
7:30 ______
8:00 ______
8:30 ______
9:00 ______
9:30 ______
10:00 ______
10:30 ______
11:00 ______
11:30 ______
12:00 ______
12:30 ______

MY EXTRAORDINARY NOTES

MY EXTRAORDINARY DAY PLANNER

M T W TH F SA SU --- JAN. FEB. MAR. APR. MAY JUN. JUL. AUG. SEPT. OCT. NOV. DEC.

1 2 3 4 5 6 7 8 9 10 11 12 13 14 15 16 17 18 19 20 21 22 23 24 25 26 27 28 29 30 31

MY TOP 4 EXTRAORDINARY PRIORITIES

- [ ]
- [ ]
- [ ]
- [ ]

EXTRAORDINARY PEOPLE

- [ ]
- [ ]
- [ ]
- [ ]
- [ ]
- [ ]
- [ ]
- [ ]
- [ ]
- [ ]

MY EXTRAORDINARY TASKS

- [ ]
- [ ]
- [ ]
- [ ]

MY EXTRAORDINARY PROJECTS

- [ ]
- [ ]
- [ ]
- [ ]

MY EXTRAORDINARY HABITS

- [ ]
- [ ]
- [ ]
- [ ]

MY EXTRAORDINARY APPOINTMENTS

5:00 __________
5:30 __________
6:00 __________
6:30 __________
7:00 __________
7:30 __________
8:00 __________
8:30 __________
9:00 __________
9:30 __________
10:00 __________
10:30 __________
11:00 __________
11:30 __________
12:00 __________
12:30 __________
1:00 __________
1:30 __________
2:00 __________
2:30 __________
3:00 __________
3:30 __________
4:00 __________
4:30 __________
5:00 __________
5:30 __________
6:00 __________
6:30 __________
7:00 __________
7:30 __________
8:00 __________
8:30 __________
9:00 __________
9:30 __________
10:00 __________
10:30 __________
11:00 __________
11:30 __________
12:00 __________
12:30 __________

MY EXTRAORDINARY NOTES

MY EXTRAORDINARY DAY PLANNER

M T W TH F SA SU --- JAN. FEB. MAR. APR. MAY JUN. JUL. AUG. SEPT. OCT. NOV. DEC.

1 2 3 4 5 6 7 8 9 10 11 12 13 14 15 16 17 18 19 20 21 22 23 24 25 26 27 28 29 30 31

MY TOP 4 EXTRAORDINARY PRIORITIES

- [ ]
- [ ]
- [ ]
- [ ]

EXTRAORDINARY PEOPLE

- [ ]
- [ ]
- [ ]
- [ ]
- [ ]
- [ ]
- [ ]
- [ ]
- [ ]
- [ ]

MY EXTRAORDINARY TASKS

- [ ]
- [ ]
- [ ]
- [ ]

MY EXTRAORDINARY PROJECTS

- [ ]
- [ ]
- [ ]
- [ ]

MY EXTRAORDINARY HABITS

- [ ]
- [ ]
- [ ]
- [ ]

MY EXTRAORDINARY APPOINTMENTS

5:00 ______
5:30 ______
6:00 ______
6:30 ______
7:00 ______
7:30 ______
8:00 ______
8:30 ______
9:00 ______
9:30 ______
10:00 ______
10:30 ______
11:00 ______
11:30 ______
12:00 ______
12:30 ______
1:00 ______
1:30 ______
2:00 ______
2:30 ______

3:00 ______
3:30 ______
4:00 ______
4:30 ______
5:00 ______
5:30 ______
6:00 ______
6:30 ______
7:00 ______
7:30 ______
8:00 ______
8:30 ______
9:00 ______
9:30 ______
10:00 ______
10:30 ______
11:00 ______
11:30 ______
12:00 ______
12:30 ______

MY EXTRAORDINARY NOTES

MY EXTRAORDINARY 30-DAY REVIEW

Week of: ______________________________

Month of: ______________________________

The "WINS" for this past week/month were:

____

____

____

What I did not get done, but intended to do:

____

____

____

Challenges, situations, and/or problems I am facing now:

____

____

____

MY EXTRAORDINARY 30-DAY REVIEW

Opportunities I see for myself right now:

What I will do before the end of this coming week/month:

Notes: